AGATHA CHRISTIE AND ALL THAT MOUSETRAP

Agatha Christie and All That Mousetrap

HUBERT GREGG

WILLIAM KIMBER · LONDON

First published in 1980 by
WILLIAM KIMBER & CO. LIMITED
Godolphin House, 22a Queen Anne's Gate
London, SW1H 9AE

ISBN 0 7183 0427 6

Typeset by Robcroft Limited, London
and printed in Great Britain by
The Garden City Press Limited
Letchworth, Hertfordshire SG6 1JS

To the onlie Mouse . . .

Contents

List of Illustrations

Acknowledgements

My gratitude to:

Chappell and Co Ltd for allowing me to quote Lorenz Hart's words from *Manhattan* . . .

Peter Maurice Music Co Ltd/EMI Music Ltd for allowing me to quote my own words from *I'm Going to Get Lit up When The Lights Go Up In London* . . .

B. Feldman and Co Ltd/EMI Music Ltd for permission to quote from the songs *Grandfather's Whiskers* and *A Marrow's A Banana's Father* . . .

Samuel French Ltd and Hughes Massie Ltd for permission to quote from the plays . . .

Rosalind Hicks for kindly agreeing to my quoting her mother's writings to me . . . Clifford Mollison for playing tennis with Gerald Du Maurier, persuading him to doctor and direct *The Ringer* – and for regaling me with related matters . . .

Phyllis Robinson – producer of my wireless programmes – for endless rearrangements of recording schedules to enable me to meet other deadlines

Finally – and most importantly, my thanks to:

Carmel Lytton for encouragement, untiring research and helpful guidelines . . . and to:

Eric Shorter for his kindness in supplying valued written contributions.

Note for Addicts

(or, I suppose, more strictly for non-addicts who haven't yet seen and enjoyed the view from the bafflement)

The presenter of *The Hollow* arranged for Jeanne de Casalis to make a mini curtain speech . . . 'You are now our partners-in-crime and we trust you to keep the secret of whodunit locked in your hearts . . .' As director, I agreed that this was on the button. Nothing more boring than to go to a whodunit with foreknowledge. I suppose you could have an evening of sorts spotting the clues . . . In the main, I'm afraid it would be a matter of 'Take away the whodunit and what have you got ?'.

At the *Mousetrap* curtain call Richard Attenborough made a similar appeal . . . 'Your friends may ask you . . . Don't tell them . . .'

I'm afraid that, from time to time in these shallow enough analyses, it will be necessary for me to go deeper and reveal whodunit in the Christie plays I directed. Four out of five of these, having come and gone, are neither here nor there. The fifth bids fair to outrun me. About this one it must be a case of 'kill and tell'. For those who may be sensitive about such disclosure I have asked the publisher to mark certain paragraphs 'STOP – Revelation Ahead'. When you spot one of these road signs . . . . simply make a detour round the paragraph/s. You won't, I assure you, have missed anything vital. Merely mortal.

Preamble

'Grandfather's whiskers, grandfather's beard!
'Never had it shingled, never had it sheared . . . '

It was on a summer afternoon in the twenties that I first became aware of Agatha Christie. She was already known as a writer of detective novels (in the thirties, an American would give them the name 'whodunits') but I was still too young to be concerned with such literary refinements. I was still with *Eric or Little by Little*.

I was young and small and skinny (except for a round face) and I spent my summer holidays at Bournemouth. Summers were mostly hot and sunny, they really were – to hell with statisticians. They were the hotter because there was no such thing – so far as I know – as lightweight clothes. Certainly for kids. I wore short trousers, called 'knickers', and woollen stockings the year round. Summer knickers could be made of grey flannel, summer jackets of blue flannel. You took your jacket off at the seaside, even your tie. But I wouldn't, at my age (ten), undress on a beach and since my weekly pocket money was fourpence a bathing hut was out of the question.

So I was to be found, attired as above described, leaning on the prom railings, absorbing every note, word and antic of Birchmore and Lindon's *Gay Cadets* – three times daily, 11.30, 3.15 and 8. (The word 'gay' had only one meaning in those days.) You didn't have to pay and sit down, you could see and hear it all for nothing, leaning. The *Cadets* sang everything that was going in the popular song line from 'Moonlight and Roses' to 'A Marrow's a Banana's Father' (a marrow's a banana's Dad, it started life as a gherkin so it hasn't done so bad). They only had to warble it once and I would know it forever.

Now it came to pass that, in those same twenties, Agatha Christie disappeared. Briefly but completely. The event made headline news and, from being a mere few-book success, A.C. exploded like a star-shell and achieved nominal household omnipresence. Some said her press agent had engineered the whole thing. It was soon to be talked of as the first ever 'publicity stunt'. It was also said that she had suffered a sad, temporary mental collapse. Whichever was true, the affair was stranger than the one 'at Styles' and Roger Ackroyd – even murdered – didn't, by comparison, get a look in. Like those sledge-hammers you try your strength with in a fair ground, that disappearance rang a bell that reverberates today. It was a mystery with no denouement.

The *Gay Cadets* had their own explanation of the adventure. There was a popular song at the time called 'Grandfather's Whiskers'. On that summer afternoon in the twenties, with me leaning, they sang it this way:

> Grandfather's whiskers, grandfather's beard!
> Never had it shingled, never had it sheared!
> Where did Mrs Christie go to when she disappeared?
> Into grandfather's whiskers, grandfather's beard!

I never forgot the name. I even read one of her books. As a boy, I mean. It was *The Murder of Roger Ackroyd*. I read it only once – you never read them twice, do you, there's no point? So I can't tell you why I remembered – vividly, if inaccurately – that the demise in the story had something to do with coffee. They did take coffee didn't they, those characters, and didn't someone say 'ooh' or something and fall down? Damn it, it is half a century ago and nothing will persuade me to pick the volume up and verify. Some mysteries –like that disappearance – had better remain unsolved.

I mention all this because my memory of coffee in connection with Ackroyd, his departure, was to cause laughter at my first meeting with Agatha Christie. Un-merry laughter. Laughter that was to colour my view of her long after I had directed her first theatre success which, it has been said, was responsible for pouring several million pounds of subsequent sterling into her pinny. (It put a thousand or two into mine but came near to damaging my career as a director beyond the point of no returns. But that's for later.)

PART ONE

CHAPTER ONE

Appearances

Appearance of Agatha Miller as a baby ... of Winston Churchill at The Mousetrap ... of a young Miss Miller in Europe, of a Torquay bride named Christie ... of Mrs Christie as a hospital dispenser among poisons, as a writer about death by poison ... as a successful writer about unnatural death in general

The life of a Duchess of Death and Wonder: how does it run . . . ?

Agatha Christie was born in Torquay, which area might be said to have tea and cucumber sandwich connotations. Comfort, warmth in winter. But right away we have a mystery. Nobody seems to know the year. It was 'probably 1891'. Natural enough, of course, for her to withhold the date. And it wouldn't have been the thing – at that time, certainly – to go rummaging about at Somerset House.* Enigma and this lady went hand in secret hand. It would have been like doing examination Latin with a crib. Or seeing *The Mousetrap* in the company of someone who had seen it before and insisted upon nudging away the delight of puzzlement. You'd feel awful verifying, you really would, let it rest. At 1891 (?), it would make her fifty-nine (?) years into crime and reward at the time of our first meeting.

She was born Agatha Mary Clarissa Miller. Let me correct that. None of us is born anything. There is that teasing moment of what-is-it speculation as we enter the world. In this case it was known with some certainty whodunit, but which set of names was going to fit? The first Miller child had been a girl born in Torquay, the second a boy born in America. The third . . . ? Clearly, Mr and Mrs Miller would have been ready – perhaps more willing – with 'Algernon Joseph Clarence'. Never mind. Hold it upside down, smack its bottom . . . (There are those about whom to imagine such goings-on sends a shudder) . . . and open the Pommery.

* In fact, Agatha's birth certificate isn't at Somerset House. It's down in Devon, away from prying eyes – now, I wonder how that was managed? And why!

Her parents had lived in Torquay since the 1880s. Father was American, mother English – or British. Such a parental mixture of bloods had given the world Winston Churchill. (He was well on in years when he paid a visit to *The Mousetrap*. And farther on in them when he confided to me his opinion. I have never breathed it to a soul, nor will I do so now except to say that he guessed who did it. Right away. There is this about Christie's work, if you have anything approaching the brain of a Churchill it isn't that difficult. Which is the reason most of us don't guess and she was a multi-millionairess.)

Her father was a simple, pleasant man by Agatha's own account and, by photographic account, one who might have doubled for King Edward VII. In looks at least. Her mother, née Clara Boehmer, had – in the phrase of the day – 'married money'. She was an arresting, forceful woman and, it seems, intuitive to the point of being clairvoyante. (Madge, the elder sister, was heard to remark that if she didn't want her mother to know a thing she wasn't even going to think it when Mama was in the room.)

Her father was more than something of an idler. (Not in the charming, Jerome K. Jerome sense.) His income derived from investments in America. These were none too wisely handled and when he died – Agatha was eleven – a little corset-tightening had to be done. (Or, I suppose, 'sash-tightening', corsets couldn't have been tighter without fatal results. *Murder by Stays* – now there's one she missed.)

Sister Madge (or 'Punkie') had been at Roedean, brother Monty at Harrow until returned to sender as not being bright enough to stay the course. (Later he entered the Army.) Mrs Miller – against her clairvoyante instincts – kept the house, Ashfield. The children had begged her not to sell. She managed, cutting three or four servants down to two or three and electing to educate her younger at home. She read to her, guided Agatha's reading and encouraged her to make up and tell stories. Here is another small mystery. Children of vivid and fast working imagination incline to gratuitous story telling to an alarming extent and have to be checked. I recall the young daughter of a friend going out into a public garden and crying quietly. When the ageing lady on the bench beside her asked what was the matter she confided that she was hungry. Her mother didn't give her enough to eat and beat her if she complained. The old lady coughed up a shilling and the ten-year-old moved off to find another sucker. That Agatha Miller who would one day – in one field – be one of our most successful story-tellers should need spurring on to fabrication is indicative of something. Slow development? Probably, merely, turn of the century reticence by the very young. (It would be nearly fifty years before children took to kicking their elders on the shins and spitting in their eye.)

Agatha Mary Clarissa studied the piano in Paris. She even did a bit of singing. The Conservatoire may or may not have been relieved when Mama whisked her off to Egypt.

In Devon, Eden Philpotts, author and playwright, was a neighbour. His Dartmoor novels – *Sons of the Morning* and *Widecombe Fair* – were well known. (He had still to stick his neck into the theatre and write the delightful and long running classic *The Farmer's Wife*. Nothing akin to *The Mousetrap* – a mere 1329 performances – but it was enough for most.) He had raging gout and wore one of those leg bandages we would see Eric Campbell sporting in Charlie Chaplin's *The Cure*. He couldn't drop in at Ashfield for tea and cucumber sandwiches even had he been disposed. The Millers did the dropping. Mrs Miller mentioned that Agatha had been busy with her pen.

'What's she been up to with it?' asked Philpotts who, despite his gout, had a turn for comedy.

'Writing,' said Mother who hadn't.

'Oh really? What?'

'Speak up,' said Mother to Agatha.

'Stories,' said the younger.

'You don't say! What are they like?'

'Sad.'

'Ah.'

Philpotts may have felt that if he didn't look out he was going to be treated to a recital. He wasn't. Nor did the shy Agatha elaborate until some years later when she described her young writings as 'stories of unrelieved gloom in which most of the characters died'.

Visitors to Ashfield in the early years included Henry James and Rudyard Kipling. No advice was sought from either.

An interesting light on the quality of Agatha's writing as it was to develop is shed by the game she played with Madge. It was Madge's invention. A 'third sister' . . . an evil non-existent. Madge would screw up her face and say to Agatha in a low, threatening voice (I would have set this in artificial light for the stage; I'm sure Madge did for the drawing room): 'Is this Madge? How do you know? I might be our older sister . . . ' etc, to the point of Agatha's wanting – joyously – to scream. Did these shenannigans plant a seed that would flower into an urge to make others scream? When reading, later when seeing and hearing?

Madge wrote stories and submitted them to magazines. They were accepted and published. More than one short story in *Vanity Fair.* Plays, too. One was actually produced by Basil Dean in London. Then Madge, like her mother, 'married money' and gave up such effort.

Agatha was recovering from 'flu when her clairvoyante Mama gave her a pad and pencil and said 'Write something'. She did. And sent it to Eden Philpotts who wrote a letter – one she treasured – setting out in some detail where she had gone wrong. She persevered and sent her stories to publishers using her grandfather's name, Nathaniel Miller. It didn't help, they came back.

At the age of twenty-one, suitably, Agatha was betrothed. The husband presumptive was Archibald Christie, a lieutenant in the Artillery who had his sights set on the Royal Flying Corps, the forerunner of the Royal Air Force. Agatha had gone up in an aeroplane in France in 1911. (It cost her mother five pounds and a mild heart attack.) She shared a love of adventure with this tall young officer, fair and curly-haired.

At that time a long engagement was considered obligatory – especially if you were of the middle class and felt you had to play by the rules. (To what extent this custom was founded upon the wisdom of gradual acquaintanceship as opposed to the desirability in a prim world of showing the lady to be in no hurry we British hazard no surmise.) The length of this engagement was obligatory for a further reason. Archibald Christie hadn't the wherewithal to support her, nor she to support him. Nobleness – and the odd emotional blow-up, occasioned no doubt by frustration – continued to put the betrothal on and off like the up-down of a gas jet. In a couple of years the war clouds had gathered. Off went Archibald to France and Agatha joined the VAD. She was posted, conveniently, to Torquay and took up duties at a Red Cross hospital.

Madge did, it seems, challenge Agatha to write a detective novel. Why this at this point? Had there been mysterious doings in Ward

Seven? Had someone swiped the digitalis? Certainly Agatha began the book while working at the hospital but, as the casualties came in, fictitious death had to wait upon the real thing.

Archie got Christmas leave and Agatha went up to London to meet him. They travelled down to his home at Clifton for the holiday. There they made a sudden decision to marry and Agatha returned to the hospital as 'Agatha Christie'.

She was moved to the dispensary where digitalis was actually to hand and the necrophiliac muse jogged her writing arm again. Finally, she took a fortnight's holiday which she spent on Dartmoor with only her muse and the ponies for company. It was her mother's idea. 'Go away and finish the book,' she had said. At the end of the two weeks Agatha came back with a completed novel called *The Mysterious Affair at Styles*. It dealt with murder by poison.

The war over, a battle was joined for publication. Anyone who has ever received a rejection slip will know that the first two dozen are the worst. The best reason, perhaps, for an author's employing an agent is that they go through somebody else's letter box. The missive to me accepting my first novel, *April Gentleman*, came out of the blue when I was rehearsing *Hamlet*. I was playing the Prince and took five after 'Get thee to a nunnery' to check through my mail. For a whole minute I couldn't make out what this letter was saying. Was it really for Ophelia? I looked at the envelope, no. After two years I had forgotten the very existence of my brain's hard-born child. Completely. You do get to that point. I was lucky in that I had other, pretty compelling interests. You don't play Hamlet every day. Or rather you do. When you do do. What I mean is, it's quite an absorbing event for the young aspirant. Happily I had had such absorption to a more or less degree for most of the two years. Not much money but plenty of absorption. And something has just occurred to me. It was indeed at this time that I was wondering whether I could afford to turn down the offer to direct Agatha Christie's *The Hollow*.

Christie's absorptions were of a domestic kind. She had given birth to a daughter, Rosalind, and was carrying on her married life in a London flat. Archie was something in the city.

It came. A letter from John Lane of The Bodley Head. She went to see him and signed a lop-sided contract which gave him a hold on her next five books. But *The Mysterious Affair at Styles* was to be published. No matter, for the moment, that it would earn her only £25. The star of the novel was Hercule Poirot, the dapper Belgian egg-head with the waxed moustache, whose intuition, born in his 'little grey cells', put him above mere clue-hunting. In *Murder For Pleasure* (Appleton-Century, 1941), Howard Haycroft wrote:

> Poirot . . . spurns the aid of science. He is the champion of theory over matter. What this postulate may lack in verisimilitude it gains in dramatic possibilities which the author knows well how to exploit to advantage.

Hercule Poirot made many a later appearance in Christie novels. Like the boys of Greyfriars he was ageless. With death all about him he was able to elude the scythe, as Harry Wharton and Co missed out on getting into the Fifth or Sixth. Charles Laughton created him on the stage but Agatha never went a bundle on seeing him come to life. 'Another Poirot?' was broached many a time and oft by publisher and manager (not by actor or director, at a guess) . . . but she stood firm in her belief that the little eccentric was best imagined. I suspect he began to bore the bloomers off her. He was, in fact, the star of *The Hollow* as a novel.

'I should never have put him in, he didn't fit,' was her own comment.

When she adapted the book for a play I had no Poirot. Thank God. I had enough problems without him. A Detective Inspector who poisons the murderer by accident is one thing but at least we didn't have him hobbling over saying, 'Drink zees'.

The Mysterious Affair at Styles did well enough. Christie took a deep author's breath and plunged into her next, *The Secret Adversary*, which was published in 1922. Now into her stride, she managed *Murder on the Links* – another 'Poirot' – by 1923. *The Man in the Brown Suit* came in 1924, *The Secret of Chimneys* in 1925. One a year was the pattern, clearly. Later it would sometimes be two. 'A Christie for Christmas' was to be a cosy catchphrase, solving the gift conundrum for many. But we are jumping like a Dartmoor pony . . .

Archie Christie had a friend named Belcher. He had been a master at Clifton and had held a wartime position of his own creating, concerning potatoes. He turned up again as one who was doing some of the organising for the British Empire Exhibition to be held at Wembley in 1924. Major Belcher – he had retained the rank – was to go round the world telling the Empire what was expected of it. Expenses paid, of course. Why didn't Archie come along as financial adviser? Expenses paid. Mrs C., too. Some expenses paid. These chances come seldom and are for the taking. Archie threw up his job, Agatha joined in the adventure, it was a highly enjoyable global romp. It landed Archie back in London without a job. But he did get another.

Adversity, in the financial way of it, never dogged their steps to the extent of tripping them. And Agatha wrote stories for magazines earning money which, surprisingly, was allowed to go straight into her pocket without sequestration by her publisher. Moreover they had only one more book coming to them before she could gain her freedom. They offered her a new contract but she had acquired an agent who was waiting to do well by her – and by himself. She submitted a quickly finished novel which she didn't like and it was turned down. Her sixth novel, *The Murder of Roger Ackroyd* (1926), had Poirot again. It also had a new publisher – Collins.

CHAPTER TWO
Disappearances

Disappearance of the Christies' marital bliss . . . 11-day disappearance of Agatha to a spa . . . Disappearance of Archie Christie's peace of mind – and of Teresa Neele's 'cover' . . . of a marriage . . . of Agatha to Baghdad and points east . . . One-day disappearance of the author.

Archie began to get restive in the London flat and announced that he was prepared to bend to Agatha's often mentioned hankering to live once more 'in the country'. Archie's hankering was for an easier life in which golf might play an ever larger part. His idea of the country was Sunningdale in Berkshire. One golf course already, another (Wentworth) planned. They saw a house which had had an 'unlucky' tag hung about it by reason of the failures of previous owners – one to hold on to his money and two others to their marriages. They bought it and, at Archie's suggestion, named it 'Styles' after the house in Agatha's first novel. A 'mysterious affair' had taken place there in Christie fiction. Another was to take place in fact at Styles. One that would astonish the country, madden the police and press, set the comedians wise-cracking and be the subject of hot debate in dwellings high and low. A mystery that would outdo any of her creation in book or on stage or screen.

Agatha's mother had died at Ashfield, and Agatha had gone down to the vast, now dilapidated, house to sort out the mountain of belongings. Archie, according to many observations by Agatha, hated illness or sorrow or trouble of any kind. A convenient view. He chose to stay at his club in London, not even joining his wife at weekends. A golf handicap is a golf handicap after all. He began seeing a lot of Major Belcher's ex-secretary Nancy Neele.

Here, the story becomes blurred. In her written mysteries Agatha Christie could always be counted on to play fair. Her scattered hints are not quite as plentiful as the red herrings but they are there. Certainly for the Churchills. About her own real life mystery she was as mum as the monkey with his paws over his mouth. If you thought of mentioning it she would ape the monkey with his ears covered. It was really as though the pictures in her mind of that disappearance were still too vivid and painful to be looked at. Hands over the eyes. In her life story,* told by herself, she doesn't even mention it. She decreed that the manuscript was to be published only after her death. 'A typical Christie ploy,' we thought. Then, when the book appeared, 'Now we shall know!' Nothing. It never happened. She does – if you search, I think – actually lay the odd red herring in our path! Force of professional habit? Or is it that, even after forty years, she was trying to deceive not us but herself?

She had every right, of course, to say nothing. This was no mere whodunit. A 'where-did-she-go-and-why' is a different kettle of deceptive fish, especially when the 'she' is you and to give direct answers would be to bare your personal bosom to public gaze. The fat, rambling (written over a period of fifteen years and sometimes charmingly) autobiography turned out to be a tapestry of cushioned living in earlier times. Petit point. No room for the grosser point of stark confession.

Her reasons for Archie's defection are thinly set out. She shouldn't have left him alone. (A pity if you can't do this to a husband.) But, in everyday writing life – before this departure with Rosalind to Devon – had she been too preoccupied with other people's vagaries to notice his? She did her thinking in the bath tub, it seems, while munching apples. More than an apple a day but not enough, surely, to keep the Colonel away if he didn't want distance. Having munched her way through to the denouement in thought, Agatha would run off a book in ten days. Closeted, of course, and deeply concentrating. Miss Neele had been a weekend guest. Was the tapping of Agatha's typewriter the signal for untrapped mice to play? But of course Agatha wouldn't have been tapping. Not with guests, that would have been, socially, against the grain. (A comparison with Edgar Wallace comes forcibly to mind. He was known for inviting a house full of them, then disappearing – there's that word again, we must watch it – into his study for the whole weekend leaving them to get on with it.)

Discretion, regarding extra-marital goings-on, was honoured

***Agatha Christie* – an autobiography, Collins, 1977

in the observance in the twenties. 'Miss Neele is our friend too,' said the hostess who invited her for a weekend party, one of whose number was Archie Christie and another of whose number was not Agatha.

The Murder of Roger Ackroyd disappointed some readers. The authoress had not played fair, they complained, in letting the story teller turn out to be the murderer. Dorothy L. Sayers, herself a writer of detective fiction (she created Peter Wimsey), felt it necessary to close ranks and spring to her defence. 'It is for the reader,' she argued, 'to suspect everybody.' Had the author come to suspect Miss Neele? Archie Christie was to state that Agatha had 'had a nervous breakdown'. Had she? Was it brought on by criticism of her writing? Does a person who is psychologically disturbed behave with the degree of exactness noticeable in the story as it developed? And what is the full story?

Agatha left home on Friday evening, 3rd December 1926. The police notice, published on Tuesday 7th December ran:

> Missing from her home The Styles, Sunningdale, Berkshire, Mrs Agatha Mary Clarissa Christie, aged 35, height 5 feet 7 inches; hair reddish and shingled, eyes grey, complexion fair, well built; dressed in grey stockinet skirt, green jumper, grey and dark grey cardigan, small green velour hat, wearing a platinum ring with one pearl. No wedding ring. Had black handbag with her containing £5-10. Left home in a Morris Cowley car at 9.45 p.m. on Friday leaving a note saying she was going for a drive. Next morning the car was found abandoned at Newlands Corner, Shere, Surrey.

We who are not police push bits of the Christie jig-saw around the table. Some fit, some don't. Some fit in more than one place. Many a piece is missing altogether.

This mysterious Friday at Styles had a normality about it if you didn't look closely. Even if you did. Agatha worked with her secretary Miss Fisher in the morning and, in the afternoon, drove to Dorking alone to have tea with relatives of the Colonel. They said she seemed 'happy and light-hearted'. (Not surprising in any circumstances that she would seem so or that they should so report.) She left them at five o'clock and arrived home at about six where she spent the evening with her husband before he went off to join the weekend party and Miss Neele.

Agatha dined alone, then went to her bedroom where she packed a small case with toiletries, a pair of slippers and an evening gown. (The last article was a little out of the ordinary, we have to feel. Especially for packing in a dressing case that, normally, would hold overnight things.) Then she scribbled a note to her secretary to the effect that she was going for 'a drive around'.

The car was what we used to call a drop-head. The hood was up, it appears, and was covered with hoar frost when the vehicle was found at Newlands Corner – which spot incidentally is on the direct way from Styles to her husband's relations at Dorking. Some reports say that the car started easily, others that the battery was flat. Some say the brakes were hard on, others that they were off.

Colonel Christie remembered that 'some time ago' his wife had had a discussion about disappearance with her sister. Agatha had contended that it was fully possible.

Naturally people came forward by the dozen to say that they had seen the missing woman . . .

An hour before dawn it was. Newlands Corner. She asked me if I could start her car. It looked as if it'd been out all night, frost all over it. All over her hair too. And she looked odd to me . . .

Milford Station – just south of Godalming. I'm a porter there. This woman – I'll swear it was her . . . very weird she looked, frost on her hat. Behaviour was strange. Asked about trains, she did. Where for? Portsmouth.

My name's Kitching. Mrs Kitching. I live in Little London, that's south of Albury. That's three or four miles from where you found the car. I saw her. About midday Saturday it was. It was her all right. She looked ever so strange – walking very slowly. Didn't ought to've been there at all, it's wild as anything on those heaths. That's where she was heading . . . . .

Frederic Doré – Alexander Road, Thames Ditton. Yes, I found the car near Newlands Corner. It had run into the bushes. I had a look inside . . . . There was a fur coat, a case and some other things. I saw this gipsy girl walking away from the car but it didn't seem she'd taken anything. The lights were on and the battery was flat. But it wasn't an accident, I mean you'd pull the brake on wouldn't you or try to stop? Brake wasn't on. Oh. And another thing, it was in neutral. Must have been pushed. Why, I wonder?

After one week – on 10th December – Colonel Christie joined in the search with Agatha's dog, a large wire-haired terrier. By 13th December two thousand people, in cars and on foot, were combing an area of forty square miles. The Silent Pool – a local beauty spot which had figured in a Christie story – had its waters dragged. (King John, it was said, had chased a maiden there. Pushed to the limit of a choice between His Majesty and the pool the poor girl had taken a header.)

The police had several pointers from Agatha herself. They displayed no Churchillian brightness about following them to a denouement. The first was a telegram telephoned by her secretary to the Ascot Exchange the night she left home. It was addressed to a Guest House in Beverley, Yorkshire, and the message ran:

REGRET CANNOT COME CHRISTIE

The second was a letter written to Madge's husband, James Watts of Cheadle, near Manchester. It told him she was ill and was on her way to 'a Yorkshire spa'. This, in fact, was where she went. But not under the name 'Christie'. She travelled to Harrogate and put up at the Hydro signing in as 'Teresa Neele'. The surname, of course, belonged to the lady Archie was pursuing in the 'Silent Pool' bit of the country. And having better luck than King John. Agatha's letter to her brother-in-law was posted in London.

Deputy Chief Constable Kenward of the Surrey Police received a letter from her too, by the second morning post on the day following her departure.* It hinted that her life was in danger and asked for help. He was giving it. On the strength of this letter and the abandoned car, he was convinced that Agatha was in the Surrey area and would be found dead. Murdered by Archie. He never wavered in this idea. Police followed Archie everywhere, they were stationed at the house, they monitored his telephone calls.

From all accounts – and there were many – Agatha presented a

* Revealed in *The Mystery of Agatha Christie* by Gwen Robyns, Penguin Books, 1979.

perfectly normal aspect to the other guests at the Hydro. She spent her time reading the newspapers, doing the crosswords and making herself agreeable. She gave them a song from time to time – which item, they considered, came into the last category. She bought clothes locally. One evening she entered the Music Room wearing a new shawl with a price label still attached. '75/-' it said. (In modern monetary terms this would amount to £3.75, qualities and value for money are not comparable. An expensive shawl.) One of the guests said, jokingly, 'Is that all you're worth?' Agatha made a solemn reply to the effect that she was worth a lot more.

Her interest in newspapers heightened on 11th December when she made an early beeline for *The Times*. She had placed a red herring in the Personal Column:

FRIENDS AND RELATIVES OF TERESA NEELE LATE OF SOUTH AFRICA COMMUNICATE—WRITE BOX 762 THE TIMES, EC4

An entertainer at the Hydro, a Miss Corbett, showed Agatha the published picture of the 'missing woman'. 'You do look like Mrs Christie,' she said.

To which Agatha replied, 'This Mrs Christie is a very elusive person but I don't want to bother with her . . . .'

Another member of the staff did however, and telephoned the police.

The news of Agatha's discovery bucked Archie Christie up like a hole-in-one. Not that he had undergone a change-back of heart. He had been the prime suspect. He didn't really want Agatha that much out of the way but he had had nightmares about trying to explain that point to a jury. The police gave him the address. He must have had a nasty turn when they told him his wife used Nancy Neele's surname. 'Don't mention it,' he said to the Inspector (meaning 'Don't tell a soul') and high-tailed it to Harrogate by the London, Midland and Scottish. His re-meeting with Agatha-Teresa Neele-Christie was described by Mr James, the Manager of the Hydro:

> It was pathetic. It happened in the lounge. The husband seated himself near the doors and, assuming an idle atititude, awaited the appearance of the guests for selection of the evening newspapers which were placed upon an adjoining table . . . .

(It occurs here that it may be a pity the matter didn't come to a trial. Mr James would have made a witness in the 'I proceeded in a north-westerly direction' mould. I wouldn't have been able to take my ears off him.)

> Mrs Christie approached and took a copy of an evening paper which contained a story of the search and a photograph of her . . . The husband immediately recognised his wife but she only seemed to regard him as an acquaintance whose identity she could not quite fix . . . .

(One wonders here whether Whoever confers the gift of writing detective novels may not perhaps throw in a modest talent for acting . . .)

> It was sufficient however to permit of her accompanying her husband to the dining room where they had dinner together.

I don't suppose it went down well. Or did it? Agatha, I was to discover, had a Gargantuan appetite. Would it permit of her feigning indifference?

After the meal, Archie cornered this Mr James. 'Not a soul,' he said, 'must know my wife registered here as "Miss Neele".'

The manager was patient. It had to be explained, however, that all the guests had been calling her 'Miss Neele' all week. 'Give us a song, Miss Neele,' they had clamoured. And 'Miss Neele' had obliged without batting an eyelid.

The press were there in force. Understandably. In other circumstances Archie might have enjoyed the limelight. Now he avoided their direct questions with extreme care. He announced that he was taking Agatha, on the morrow, to see a specialist in London. He thanked the press – and police – publicly for their untiring efforts to find his wife. He ended with a plea that they should now be left undisturbed.

Madge and her husband James Watts arrived the next morning and shepherded Agatha and Archie to the back door and out into a conveyance. (A smart photographer managed to scoop a picture of Agatha, cloche-hatted, slinking through the gateway.) At the station, James Watts bought the tickets and the quartet made its way

Birchmore and Lindon's *Gay Cadets*. They performed on Bournemouth beach (on a stage but the stage was on the beach) at the foot of the West Cliff lift. It was from them that I first heard the name Agatha Christie.

Agatha as a young girl.

to the train. Agatha locked herself in the compartment with Madge – Archie and James taking it in turns to stand guard outside the door. At Leeds they changed for Manchester where a waiting car carried them to the Watts' home, Abney Hall, Cheadle. The gates were locked behind them as they were driven in.

The following day, Archie issued this statement to the Press:

> My wife is extremely ill, suffering from complete loss of memory. Three years have dropped out of her life. She cannot recall anything that has happened during that period . . . .

(What about the name 'Neele'? What about the words of the songs she sang in the music room at the Hydro? But this was a prepared statement – no questions.)

> The fact that she lives at Sunningdale has no significance for her and she does not seem to realise that her home is 'Styles'. As to what happened since she left there her mind is a complete blank. She has no recollection of going to Newlands Corner or of proceeding eventually to Harrogate. As is only to be expected she is very upset as a result of the journey yesterday and has no idea what all the fuss is about. She now knows who I am and has also realised Mrs Watts is her sister. It is somewhat remarkable that she does not know she has a daughter. In this connection she was shown a picture of herself and Rosalind, her little daughter. She asked who the child was. What was the child like? How old was she?
>
> My wife has been seen today by a local doctor and this afternoon a specialist from Manchester will see her for further consultation. I tell you this in order that you will respect my feelings and not worry the specialist or myself. All the worry has been terrible and all we want now is peace and quietness. I have been offered £300 [Another newspaper had it at £500] to tell how my wife came to Harrogate. I do not know and she cannot tell me.

The literary style was pretty ordinary but it was all the world was going to get in the way of explanation.

There was also a medical statement – clearly authorised, perhaps encouraged, by Archie Christie:

> After a careful examination [not a sloppy one, mind] of Agatha Christie this afternoon, we have formed the opinion that she is suffering from an unquestionably genuine [strange phrase] loss of memory and that, for her future welfare, she should be spared all anxiety and excitement. Signed Donald Core, M.D., Henry Wilson MRCS.

Archie added a request to the public to keep away from Abney Hall so that his wife could have the benefit of fresh air. Then, astonishingly, he said that he refused to consider himself responsible for the expenses incurred by the police in their search for his wife. He added that he always knew that Agatha was alive and had never, in fact, asked the police to begin a search. (One in the eye for Deputy Chief Constable Kenward who had made him Suspect Number One.)

Kenward announced that he had received a number of letters containing money – in some cases large amounts – to help defray the cost of the ten days' search for Mrs Christie. He had returned all the money and asked that no more be sent. Sir Arthur Spurgeon, a member of the Surrey Standing Joint Committee responsible for Police expenditure, said that the matter had been exaggerated. Somebody had, he said, estimated the cost to be the equivalent of a penny on the rates. This would work out at about £25,000. Sir Arthur said it would be nearer £25. (2,000 people over 40 square miles – a modest price. We imagine there would be a predominance of amateur sleuthery. But how much would it cost to drag a Silent Pool?) He added that Colonel Christie had said all along that he would cover the cost. A bill had been sent. (There is some evidence to support his having settled it. Was Archie buying peace and quiet?)

Miss Nancy Neele was not available for comment. Ever.

The newspapers doubted the 'loss of memory' story. For certain specified reasons:

1. A woman who has lost her identity would not have been able to obtain the money to take her to Harrogate. (But travel was cheaper then and Agatha had up to ten pounds in her handbag. In 1926 you could sail to New York and back for £35.)

2. The choice of the name of a friend (sic) for a pseudonym was not consistent with loss of memory. (A hard one.)

3. The announcement inserted in *The Times* asking friends of Teresa Neele to communicate was not consistent with loss of memory, whereas it is consistent with another theory.

(Even harder. What theory? I suppose they couldn't elaborate. Was it a code message to anyone in the know, telling them how to communicate?)

4. Mrs Christie's appearance and bearing during the last few days were not those of a sick woman.

Archie's reply was a simple reiteration of all he had said before. No specific answer to any one question given.

The loose ends . . . . . As fast as you tie one up another drops free. The London postmark on Agatha's letter to her brother-in-law . . . ? Had she given the letter to a friend to post, had she travelled to London? (I can't, I must confess, see Agatha – covered in hoar frost – hitching a lift from Newlands Corners to Harrogate. If she travelled there by rail she would, surely, have to start from London.) How did Agatha pay for both the journeys and for the new clothes? Just how far would ten pounds carry you in 1926? It was a large enough sum. She would not have paid anything at the hotel until the end of her stay.

If Agatha did go to London she might have done better to linger. Nothing like a few nights on the town to take your addled mind off mysterious goings-on in the country. A glance at a theatre list would have told her that *Rose Marie* was in her second year at Drury Lane. Too innocent for the mood? *Lady Be Good* – with the Astaires – at the Empire? (The title rang like an appeal to Nancy Neele. Or to Teresa?) For looking on the bright side, *Sunny* – with Jack Buchanan – was at the Hippodrome . . . . *The Co-Optimists* at His Majesty's . . . . At the Winter Garden – where she would have a smash hit of her own some thirty years later, *Tip Toes*. Innocence again. The title of the play at the St James's might have depressed her – *The Last of Mrs Cheyney* . . . . She might have been sorry she ditched the car on reading that petrol had been reduced to one and fivepence halfpenny from the pump . . . . . Then again, she might have been relieved, reading that Leslie Henson, the actor, had been fined a second time for speeding (he had driven at thirty-four miles an hour in Regent's Park) . . . . . If she fancied a booze-up to forget Miss Neele – or to remember her for an entry in some hotel register – whisky was twelve and six a bottle or 62½p. (It was still twelve and six a bottle twelve years later; inflation didn't exist outside Germany.) Champagne cost the same . . . brandy (for rich authors only) cost fourteen and six (72½p.). A bottle.

The telegram to the other hotel (REGRET CANNOT COME CHRISTIE) . . . . The question to the porter about a train to Portsmouth . . . In a play they would seem to be clumsily laid red herrings. The car – left as though there had been an accident . . . Clumsiness . . . . does it allay suspicion . . . .? Or foster it . . . ? The police seem to have been happy with the loss of memory theory. The doctors too, they would have had no axe to grind. Or would they? 'The lady says she doesn't feel well . . . . she must rest . . . Mr Christie? Ah yes, as you say, peace and quiet . . . '

A word for poor Archie Christie. So he was a womaniser. Many a husband who is wouldn't be if he was man-ised by his wife. The Jameses who invited him, with Nancy Neele, for that week-end clearly thought he was in need of sympathy. We were to learn they were the only guests. He was popular enough with the men around him – with whom, often, Agatha was not so popular. Whatever his faults, it may be felt that the punishment meted out to him by Agatha was pretty cruel. She set out deliberately – the facts shout it – to throw murder suspicion upon him. She, meanwhile, was up north, having a high old time playing the popular girl at the Harrogate Hydro. She even danced the Charleston.

Daily, she checked the newspapers – to see what hell Archie was going through? One newspaper mentioned Agatha's love of adventure. It reminded its readers of her novel *The Secret Adversary* . . . Agatha had dedicated it to:

> All those who lead monotonous lives, in the hope that they may experience at second hand the delights and dangers of adventure.

When, at last, she was rumbled and a cub reporter – Ritchie Calder, no less! – asked her point blank, 'Are you Mrs Christie?' she came back with a line of dialogue that simply won't do. Had it occurred in one of her plays I would have nipped it before we got into rehearsal. 'Yes,' she said. 'But I'm suffering from amnesia.' Two weeks earlier she had left a diamond ring on the counter at Harrods during a shopping bout. She wrote from Harrogate asking them to send the ring to her care of Miss Teresa Neele at the Hydro. This personal play she was writing mentally was full of un-Christie-like holes, that's the most you could say in favour of an identity change.

Just what did Agatha expect to achieve? Did she think Archie would be filled with remorse as well as terror at the prospect of the gallows? Did she think that, on learning that she was alive, he would react like a child caught with fingers reaching for the larder shelf? That he would come running back to her, dropping Nancy Neele like a stolen hot cookie?

I dismiss at once the protest that Agatha Christie didn't need the publicity. She had written five successful books. She was becoming known. (But – to one major newspaper – slowly. They headlined their story 'A Woman Novelist'.) Her sixth book had been issued only recently. She was with a new publisher. I would say this was the perfect moment for a big boost. And, on a publicity level alone, what a boost it turned out to be! What greater sensation could you have than a writer of mystery stories who becomes the central character in one herself?

Innocent people suffered. If Agatha thought Archie irresponsible, she was outdoing him by leagues. Poor Deputy Chief Constable Kenward, to whom she had written so convincingly for help, was not to know he hadn't a chance against this queen of deception. He was never to forget what he regarded as his failure in duty. Before he died – in his mid-fifties – he gave instructions to his daughter, a police worker, to burn all the correspondence relating to the case.

Her personal adventure concluded – though the buried story would continue to squirm under earth that covered it but loosely, Agatha re-joined the ranks of the living. The ensuing two years must have been barely tolerable for the restless, trouble-hating Archie. Appearances had to be kept up. Miss Neele had to be put on ice, so to speak. He had no intention of forgetting her; she was a creature comfort. The possibility that the continuing liaison might send his wife off on her travels again didn't shake him. Miss Neele remained as firmly in his mind as she had in the mind, conscious or subconscious, of the wandering Agatha.

Mrs Christie records that she gave the Colonel every opportunity to fall in and go through the drill of being a happy husband and father. Archie didn't even make it to the parade ground. He went AWOL at last, Styles was sold, its mystery still intact . . . Only marriage was to undergo a denouement. The divorce happened in 1928. The reticent Miss Neele whose name Agatha had annexed for ten days now became 'Mrs Christie' for life.

Agatha threw herself into travel. She declared her revulsion against the press (who didn't care for inconclusivity) and shot off – on her Tod Sloane – to Baghdad. (Where else?) On the way she was all but murdered by bed bugs. Later she penned a novel about the train – the Orient Express. The murder – not by bed bugs – was solved on the screen by Albert Finney disguised as Hercule Poirot.

In 1930, during a visit to Muqaiyir in Iraq (she did get about), she met Max Edgar Mallowan – a man fourteen years her junior. Mallowan was assisting Sir Leonard Woolley in the excavations that were to lead to a kindly light being shed upon the ancient Sumerian city of Ur. They married and Agatha began yearly trips, accompanying him to Iraq and Syria. She tabulated for him and even took photographs. While she was waiting for him to dig up something else she would dash off the occasional book. Life – in proximity to ancient death – took on a new meaning. And new royalties. *Murder in Mesopotamia* (1936), *Death on the Nile* (1937) and *Appointment with Death* (1938) kept her publisher happy.

During the Second German War, Mallowan was in Tripolitania as adviser to the British Government on Arab affairs. Agatha was at University College in London – in the dispensary again. After the war it was back to the ruins for both Mallowans, Assyrian ruins this time. Rummaging among the seventh century left-overs. Or left-unders. Agatha was reported as saying that she found searching for clues more fascinating than laying them. (I wonder how she would have made out in December 1926 if Archie had been the lost one and she on the searching side. I'll bet she wouldn't have bothered to wet her waders in the Silent Pool.)

The hue and cry over the disappearance was an unconscionable time a-dying. Agatha – perhaps because of her chosen new way of life with its scholarly companionship and its annual retreat to the tombs – was no longer front page news. But the aura remained. At our first meeting, in 1950, the 'happening' sprang at once to mind. Did it – does it still? – spring to the mind of a bookshop browser seeing her name on a jacket? The effect of it upon the sales of her novels was assessable only by those privy to the figures. Newspapers rushed to serialise her stories (at a guess, she felt no revulsion at this).

Every writer of detective fiction in the 1926/7 English-speaking world must have – in thought – broken the commandment that deals with one's neighbour's bits and pieces – his ass and what not. 'Thou shalt not covet thy neighbour's disappearance . . . ' If they had husbands, these authors – or wives, the chat behind the blinds may have run:

'Why can't *you* find a "Miss Neele" then, it can't be that difficult?'

'What would you do if I did?'

'Do? Hit the millionaire bracket, that's what!'

Or:

'Why can't *you* find a man to go off with, Archie Christie did it?'

'Found a man?'

'No! He found a woman but there's nothing to stop my wife losing her memory.'

'You think that would get your book published?'

'All eight of 'em. We'd be set for life. Who do you know, now . . . ?'

Would the owners of these imaginary voices have pointed an accusing finger? Or thought 'There, but for the luck of the devil . . .'? Would they have felt a pang of sympathy for the troubled wife or saluted a 'sly old fox'? Writers as they were and students of the human psyche they would have been the first to re-shape the scene had it been played for publicity. They would have left out the reference to Miss Neele. It would have been quite out of character for Agatha to have displayed soiled linen for gain. But then . . . might not such a mistress of deception . . . deceive? Surely it is the unexpected we are to expect? So that, in the end, the expected may turn out to be the true answer? (I've directed too many whodunits, we must take something at face value or go mad!)

I am going, at this point, to tell of a happening in my own life. I have never spoken of it to a soul, certainly not written it down. But it seems to me to be apposite.

In 1955 I was under an almost intolerable strain for a period of weeks. The reasons are private. In a lowered physical and mental condition, I was overworking to a ludicrous degree. I was writing, appearing on BBC Television as Chairman of the Brains Trust and rehearsing for the Sunday night production of an American drama in which I was playing the leading character. He had a hell of a lot to say and, to make matters depressing, he was dead at the beginning of the play. He was, in fact, the ghost of himself, moving among the friends and enemies he had left behind. I mentioned depression but it didn't upset me. The part was so good that I was enjoying the rehearsals. In my subconscious, yes, I may have been affected by the funereal aspect – at one point he was present at the undertaker's while his widow is discussing his burial! It would be true to say that, what with one private matter and another, I was becoming the ghost of myself while getting into the dead mind of this man.

I was due to rehearse at the Strand Theatre on the Saturday morning before the Sunday performance. On the Sunday, I had arranged for myself a hair-brained schedule. I was to dress-rehearse this dead man all day, be hustled away by car to the television studios for a camera rehearsal, then the show – an early evening programme . . . then, by fast car, back to the Strand Theatre in time to go straight on the stage . . . having thought myself into death!

Early on the Saturday morning I got out my car and drove to Eastbourne. I had been there a week earlier, looking at property. I was conscious of every single move I made but was quite incapable of control. It was as though another person were inhabiting my body and acting not according to my intent but to his own.

Having reached the town, I drove along the sea front in the direction of Beachy Head. I don't know to this moment what my purpose was. I was outside myself –watching my own behaviour. I drove – not at any great speed – up the hill, following the sign posts. I couldn't find the way. It would have been simple for me if I had had it in mind to walk, the directions were quite clear for walkers. I just couldn't discover the route for a car . . . I drove round for about twenty minutes, then gave it up. I was drained of all energy, I had to rest. I drove back towards the town and stopped a little way down the hill. I left the car at the roadside and went to a bench on the grass. I loosened my tie, stretched out on the seat and looked up at the sky. I had been there for about an hour when a police car pulled up and two policemen came over to me. I began to panic, as though I had been caught committing some crime. But they were infinitely kind. They knew my name, someone had telephoned from

London . . . They asked me to go with them. In the car one of them asked me what I was doing at that particular spot? I could only answer that I didn't know. Had I thought of suicide, he asked. I didn't know that either. Whether the force that was directing me had thought of it . . . There were no answers.

A car came from London and friends took me home. I was put to bed and had a visit from a doctor. Everybody was memorably kind and patient. The doctor said that I must not bother with the television engagement but that I must, at all costs, try to appear in the play. I think he sensed a rising panic in me about the play. The television programme was routine. The play was something very special to me; I made him see that. Very forcibly, I learned afterwards. The BBC received the news with mixed feelings. If I could appear in a play, surely I was able to appear for them? The doctor was put on to them. I don't know what he said to them but they agreed to release me for that programme.

I rehearsed like an automaton all next day. The other actors, I sensed, had been told something. I don't know what, but they kept a distance and were quietly helpful. I had better be good in the part after all this, I remember thinking. (I had begun to take over again! I felt like one who had been held under water but has managed to surface in time.) It needed a supreme effort to begin. The curtain rose on me looking down on my own corpse . . . standing outside . . . standing outside a dead self. But I was alive . . . alive, merely playing dead. As I began to speak – to a self no longer mine – a feeling of relief flooded over me and through me . . .

The mind can play such tricks. If such a thing happened to you, you know and understand. The circumstances – the motivations – were not similar. The exactness of behaviour, the willingness to make social contact with people unconnected with whatever one is running away from . . . (I was found by my friends sitting in the Chief Constable's garden, having tea in the sun – normality itself – they were almost disappointed!) . . . these tallied.

There are other parallels worth examining. I 'disappeared' for a day only – less. I remember though, quite clearly, that I cursed the necessity for going back to the play. *I wanted to go farther, stay longer.* (Anyone can stand in for a Brains Trust Chairman I reasoned, logically. The play was more important. I actually wanted to get back to the character – if only the single performance could be delayed by, say, a week.) On this point the controlling force would not override me but I remember the clarity of my thinking and the strength of the contra-impulsion. It was a pull like death itself. Is a week the requisite term for the mind to take a holiday?

I suppose had I, at the wheel, had my way and gone farther – for longer . . . I might have been in the newspapers, almost certainly I would have been. I was known in the theatre and other media of entertainment – perhaps to the same extent that Mrs Christie was known in detective fiction after six books and before her disappearance. If the press had splashed my name about the country they would have done so whether such splashing had been my intention or not. Would I have been accused as Agatha was of disappearing into grandfather's whiskers for gain? Would I have laid red herrings – unconscious or subconscious? (Not, in my place, conscious – I am able to know. About Agatha I can only surmise.) Would I have registered in the name of the dead man in the play? Or as 'Julian Huxley'? Or in the name of one who had caused my mind to bend? I can only thank the kindness of those who, like me, stood outside the matter and enabled me to re-enter myself with the minimum of fuss.

PART TWO

CHAPTER THREE

Baptisms

How to guess whodunit . . . Baptism of Gerald Du Maurier as doctor/director . . . Baptismal dunkings of a commercial manager . . . Fiery baptism of the author as doctor/director/economist . . . Divorce mothers necessity . . . An agent tries hard but I still get the job . . . The importance of Grandfather's whiskers.

Following her disappearance in the twenties, Agatha Christie became compulsory whodunit reading. Overnight she had been catapulted on to the lap of every feeder upon such fiction from Torquay to Toronto, from Melbourne to Massachusetts. (Her considerable income from America was not even, at that time, subject to tax.) Her publishers were up to their necks in reprint after reprint. After reprint. Archie Christie had put distance between himself and a gold mine.

It was boasted – and it proved to be true – that her books were translated into more languages than Shakespeare. (I have wondered what they made of Lady Angkatell in the Netherlands Antilles. Or Michael Starkwedder. Or even Roger Ackroyd.)

To meet a person who has never read an Agatha Christie is to be back in the world of the famous Bateman cartoons. To meet one who has re-read her would be to undergo the same transport. The books make perfect train journey material. The propagation of Agatha Christie would, in itself, justify the coming of the paperback. I've seen them in Portugal, I've seen them in Peru. The QE2, I can state for a fact, sells them on at least five of the seven seas. I've noticed them on offer at airports from Heathrow to San Diego, from Kennedy to Orly, from Cologne to Muscat to Kuala Lumpur. I didn't find one in China, but then I wasn't looking. I found one in Japan. Agatha Christie is a peruser's must, has been ever since grandfather felt that stirring in his whiskers.

The characters in Christie's books are not so much stock as clever extensions of the stock. They are highly coloured, they need to be for each must catch the eye of the reader as just the piece he is looking for to complete the jig-saw. Sometimes the character is *deceptively* grey. Your attention is drawn because, as a whodunit-worker-out, you are astute enough to follow un-obvious leads up the garden. Mrs Christie knew her craft as Houdini knew his knots.

Once I tried to get to the bottom of her lethal mathematics. During rehearsals for *The Hollow*, Peter Saunders who was presenting it came up with an idea that appeared to hold water. 'The murderer is the one first on the scene after the murder,' he said. For *The Hollow* it held good but when we read *The Mousetrap* we had to think again. A useful hint – assuming that you could use one – is that a stupid character is often made to come out with the truth. 'I think it's the wife,' says the clottish police sergeant in *The Hollow*. (He was played by Shaw Taylor who stayed with crime and was to have more attention paid to him.) The Inspector looks at him pityingly and – wrongly, of course – we dismiss the wife as a suspect.

STOP

Revelation Ahead

Another feeling advanced was that it is the absolute impossibility who did it. This is quite a good one. Mind you, every whodunit writer must aim at the idea of your considering the culprit an impossibility. But Christie makes assurance trebly sure. In *Ten Little Niggers* the villain gets – don't we see it with our own eyes? – knocked off while we are on our way to the denouement. Not bad. In *The Mousetrap* the culprit is the detective sergeant who is doing the investigating – I mean, you don't stand a hope. In *The Unexpected Guest* we may not, again, believe our eyes since Starkwedder enters to find a dead man having bumped him off before the curtain went up. A bit of a cheat, this, I did think. But we ran for six hundred and four performances.

I'm anticipating entrances. I am speaking of the Christie plays when, in fact, she didn't write any for an unconscionable time. She was content to write a book or so a year ('A Christie for Christmas, my publisher expects it') and to live the life of a Duchess. And why not? I can think of few people who gave, over the decades, so much intense – if brief and concentrated – pleasure. Even in the Netherlands Antilles.

As far as the theatre whodunit was concerned, in my day the

master was Edgar Wallace. I read more Wallace than I ever did Christie. When he was transferred to the stage the theatricality that was generally acceptable to public in the twenties and thirties suited his form to an innocent T. *The Ringer* was memorable. It was first-class melodrama with a superb surprise at the end. 'Where are you Meister, the Ringer has come to get you' – spoken in the dark – made a bigger dent in this kid than dry old Shaw hooting, 'How long, oh Lord, how long?' through the puppet lips of his St Joan.

That moment in *The Ringer* had me so far on the edge of my seat it was a wonder I didn't topple off that steep gallery at the Lewisham Hipp. and land knickers-up in the Fauteuils. (That's what they called them – just on the box office board; nobody ever said anything but 'stalls'.) And it wasn't only the eagerness to know at last to whom that voice belonged. The play was high melodrama. The very telling of a mystery story lent itself to melodrama and Wallace was the best. Today the theatregoer has come to expect more subtlety. I think. Certainly, panels don't slide open and shut as frequently as they did in my school days. Wigs and whiskers are no longer whipped off at denouements. A pity. These once highly acceptable frolics have been replaced by boring detectives who question endlessly and lead us up the verbal rather than visual garden. Then they turn out to be the murderer, God help us!

Revelation Ends

When Edgar Wallace was persuaded to put *The Ringer* on the stage it had to be realised that a writer of successful mystery novels is not, ipso facto, a potential author of plays that run. Whether Wallace knew this or had it pointed out to him is not on record. He did have a go at turning his book into a play. The management – sometimes they do strike with genius – engaged Gerald du Maurier to direct. Du Maurier, a distinguished 'natural' actor, happened also to be a first class play doctor. (As a matter of fact, any director worth his salt should be something of a writer, it helps no end.) Du Maurier read Wallace's draft and stated categorically that he, du Maurier, would undertake the direction of *The Ringer* only if given a free hand to rewrite wherever and whenever he thought necessary. Wallace may have jibbed, I suspect not. Further, du Maurier asked for – and received – a substantial percentage for his creative contributions to the script.

Wallace sat at the back of the stalls throughout rehearsals of *The Ringer* watching and listening while du Maurier took his work and moulded it to the new medium. It was, for the time, a superb adaptation. And it was a smash hit. When it had been running for some weeks Wallace sent du Maurier a cheque for seven thousand pounds with a note saying, 'It's cheap at the price'.

I tell the story as an example of *'autre temps, autre moeurs'*!

What draws them in? This is the thought in the mind of every theatre manager who isn't subsidised by the Arts Council of Great Britain. Those who are may be tempted to be adventurous at public expense. The morality of this is open to question but nobody seems to query. 'It depends,' you say, 'what you mean by adventurous. Are new authors, new directors not to be encouraged?'

When Peter Saunders decided to present *The Hollow* he was, in effect, doing both. Without public money in support. I had never directed a play in London and Christie was pretty new in theatre-land. Her longest run had been *Ten Little Niggers*. (In later, more permissive, years the title was disallowed. The play was renamed *Ten Little Indians*. Who cares about Indians?) These lads performed two hundred and sixty times. Not bad for the St James in 1943? (But London was full of smash hits!) Nonetheless, eight years later, with no Indians in between, you could say Christie was an unknown quantity in the theatre.

What draws them in? Binkie Beaumont of H.M. Tennent plumped for star actors and actresses; no other management could get a look in. Moreover Saunders, being in a modest way, couldn't really afford to hire them. He decided to go for a name author. He presented, on tour, a play called *The Poison Belt* but discovered that, far from drawing them in, Conan Doyle kept them out. Or maybe Keneth Kent and I kept them out, we were both in the play.

The coffers were all but empty and Saunders put out a tour of minimally paid actors in a play called *Black Coffee*. The author – the only 'name' on the bill – Agatha Christie. It made money. Enough to convince Saunders that here was a potentially drawing author. Could he get hold of a new play by her? Having done so, could he persuade a name actor or two to appear in it? First things first.

At that time, the end of the forties, Agatha Christie had one theatre patron. By name, Bertie Meyer. She wasn't entirely happy with the forward march of her theatrical career under his aegis but

Agatha and her daughter Rosalind.

Archie Christie.

Nancy Neele—from the portrait by Richard Jack.

nobody else seemed to be falling over themselves to present her plays. Saunders approached her agents, Hughes Massie. Softly catchee Christie seemed to be the order. Old Patience on that monument could have made nothing like the nether imprint. At last Christie who had avowed loyalty to Bertie Meyer (he had presented her first – *Alibi*) said that if he didn't put on her latest within six months Saunders might have it. (I can't think who else would've, so I don't feel there was any over-generosity involved.) Her latest was an adaptation – by her – of her novel *The Hollow*. Saunders waited. Bertie Meyer dillied. Hughes Massie rang up and said:

'Saunders, it's yours.'

A friend of Peter Saunders had seen a Sunday night production of mine at the Globe, called *Potter's Notch,* a first class, Brigadooney American comedy, damned difficult, which I loved directing. I was proud of the result. It brought Peter to another play I directed – again, for a Sunday night – at the Whitehall (in days before it became branded as the home of broadish comedy). This was *Sing Cuckoo* by Judy Campbell, a super romp about ladies whose men were away at the Crusades. I put in music (I think I even wrote some!) and did quite a bit of choreography. The first act was hysterically funny but the second act couldn't top it. It was merely hilarious. I still don't know why no management bought it – with a little re-writing they would have had a smash hit. The tragedy about single-performance productions is that you have no 'next night' in which to correct anything.

Peter mentioned he was sending out a tour of a farce starring Ralph Lynn. Hadn't got a director. Upon this hint I spake and agreed to direct the piece – and do quite a bit of doctoring – for an all-in payment of twenty-five pounds. I was keen. Moreover the opportunity to work with the greatest farceur of our time was not to be missed. Had my employer but known, I would have undertaken the job for nothing. (I must add here that this was not a reasonable attitude. I was being taken for a punishing ride by divorce lawyers and hadn't a bean I could, with any certainty, call my own. I had worked hard and successfully for many years and there was a prevalent idea that I was well-heeled. I suspect Saunders thought so. I know for paper-fact that the lawyers thought so. Nevertheless I still say that I would have directed Ralph Lynn for nothing. It was to be an education and a joy in the light of which money had no meaning.)

It was necessary for me to exercise economy on my employer's behalf in this production and I think I was able to be helpful. We had a ready-made set that didn't in any way suit the room I had in mind. There was a large fireplace upstage centre for one thing. Fireplaces are items people are inclined to face which meant the audience would, if I moved the players with any kind of realism, be looking at bottoms.

'What are you going to do?' asked my boss.

'Simple,' I said. 'Whip out the fireplace.'

'That,' he said, 'will leave a whacking great hole; what do you do about the hole?'

'Stick a cabinet in front of it,' I answered.

These devices – and many another – worked well and the production made a little money. To mount productions lavishly, using a million or more of public funds, and wind up showing a deficit is easy. To create – within a careful budget – a commercial project that shows a profit is, I maintain, commendable and professional. The secret is to know the difference between economy and cheese-paring. When to paddle in the shallows and when to splash right out. In the case of the great showmen like Charles B. Cochran, you add the flair that leads you to a disregard of all the rules. And into bankruptcy. As I've hinted earlier, I don't think much of money. It isn't, let me say, a thing I remember. Not with affection, anyway. I shall always remember Cockie.

Then, one day, I was given the script of *The Hollow* to read. It was hair-raising. I don't mean it raised my hair as *The Ringer* had raised it at the Lewisham Hipp. I mean I thought it abysmal. The dialogue was unspeakable. Or, to say the least, uncharacteristic. (Example:

HENRIETTA: Hurry up, Henry, it's nearly dinner time.
HENRY (Colonial Governor type): I'll be like greased lightning.)

The characters were caricatures. The denouement was good. I was surprised to learn whodunit but by the time I got there I didn't bloody well care. 'Jesus,' I said to myself quietly. 'I need the job,' I said. (Endeavouring to surface from this divorce was like a drowning man coming up through seaweed.) 'I'm longing to direct a play in London. But are the need and the longing this bad? Will a hot bath and a telephone call and a dinner for two and a bottle and what not drive it out of my system?'

Jesus.

Saunders rang.

'What do you think?'

'Er . . . ' I began. 'Er . . . ' I went on. 'It's . . . er . . . not that bad. Denouement's good.'

'That's what I thought,' he contributed.

'It wants work on it,' I said. 'Question is how amenable is the old bird to a bit of rewriting?'

'Rewriting how much?'

'Oh, I don't know. The play?'

Saunders rode over that one. I had a suspicion he was in agreement.

'I've asked her to lunch,' he said. 'Next week. You come. Use your charm but don't say anything I'll regret. I've bought the play.'

Jesus.

In the interim we sketched out a bit of casting. We stumbled at once on a snag. Christie's characters, when you put them on a stage become flashy. By which I mean they hit you like Day-Glow. (If you don't remember, this was a clever invention that enabled the painted word on a poster to come at you like a Plastogram. If you don't remember, this was a cinema trick. They dished out glasses as you went in and somebody threw something at you from the screen and it all but hit you in the eye.) Each one, for reasons already mentioned, is designed to catch the attention and hold it. Each is a 'star part'. No sooner is one star discarded as a suspect however, than he or she takes a header into limbo. Consider Veronica in *The Hollow*. She makes an entrance that Dietrich wouldn't scorn at the end of Act One. How many people hate Dr John Cristow and could have a motive for doing him in? Veronica is the cherry on the who's-going-to-do-it Knickerbocker Glory. She is – who would have guessed? – a film star who lives – where? – up the road. (Or across the cow pasture.) She has heard the doctor is here and arrives, not at the front door but at the French window (No! Yes!).

Who is going to play Veronica? An actress who looks stunning, could hold her own with Bette Davis, can stop a stage cold merely setting foot on it . . . who hasn't yet, despite all this, been snapped up even by British films . . . and who doesn't mind the fact that her character peters out like last year's candle in this year's power cut. Multiply this situation by about eight and you have our problem as we began to cast. Every character, with the exception of the constabulary and the maid, is an inflated doll whose air gets let out as the play progresses. They have to be depicted by folk who see the pitfalls and are experienced enough either not to disappear into them or to climb out pretty adroitly if they do. But experienced folk – and folk with some sort of theatre name – are usually wily enough not to be put to such tests. Unless, of course, they need the money.

Saunders had succeeded – for whatever reason – in attracting Jeanne De Casalis to the part of Lady Angkatell. Jeanne had made a success on the wireless as 'Mrs Feather' but was also an accomplished theatre performer. Lady A. was to give her a chance to combine the two. She was to drive us all up the wall but – in the last analysis – was to be as important to the success of *The Hollow* as anybody.

Came the task of finding a Dr Cristow. He makes quite a star impression does Cristow. In Act One. And in the first scene of Act Two. Then his wife expresses her boredom ballistically and down goes the star on his belly. So. Who is going to play a character who makes a deep impression on the audience for half a play, then a deeper one on the carpet? Someone who wants to catch up on his reading? A fallen star? A rising star? Or someone who needs the money?

One afternoon an agent – who had been trying like mad to sell another director to Saunders but had lost – rang me to say that Saunders 'certainly had a yen to use me' and was on his way round. 'What do you mean?' I asked, reasonably, since he stood to get ten per cent of the bread. The answering voice was angry, it really was (was my ten per cent going to be worth less than the ten per cent of the other director he was pushing? Probably.) 'I promised not to say. He's on his way round.' This is an agent? I thought to myself. I prepared to receive my boss.

'How do you feel?' asked Saunders, 'about directing *and* playing Cristow?'

'Both at once?' I asked. (I didn't know what I meant either.)

'Not a thing I would suggest ordinarily,' said Saunders. 'But he does die in Act Two.'

'I had noticed,' I said.

'Meaning you don't think it's a good enough part?' he said.

'Any actor,' I said, 'of any consequence,' I said, 'who would accept Cristow if he didn't need the money would be out of his histrionic mind.'

'Will you play it and direct?' he asked. (Clearly he thought I either did or was, if you can work that out.)

I did a quick bit of mental arithmetic. It was my first London production. My already agreed percentage was minimal. The salary for Cristow wouldn't be maximal – I could see that coming a mile off. The two together, however, might constitute a living wage. And there was that letter from my ex-wife's solicitor. Even so, I'm proud to say I hesitated.

'I'll co-star you with Jeanne . . . ' This sly sop to the ego knocked the coconut out of its cup and there I was.

'One thing,' said Saunders. 'Christie doesn't know, we mustn't spring it on her. She's never heard of you.'

'I didn't disappear into grandfather's whiskers, that's why,' I said, a little heatedly. Saunders looked puzzled.

'Let's get it straight,' I said. 'Does Christie know I'm directing?'

'It's been mooted. Depends on the lunch, you must use your charm.'

'You said that,' I said.

CHAPTER FOUR

Hollow Laughter

Agatha Christie eats me for luncheon at the Carlton (no black coffee) . . . 'Hollow' laughter . . . Wisdom of 'Feather'–ing our nest . . . Laughter of Lord Mountbatten . . . Bad business over a sofa (retired) . . . I get a surprising pat on the back and turn down an invitation to become a millionaire.

The Carlton was the venue. It isn't there any longer. I met Saunders early in the bar. He was spruce and bristling with nerves, we both were.

'I've told the barman,' he said, 'to bring doubles every time I order singles.'

'Christie a bit of a boozer?' I asked.

'No, you fool. They're for us. Don't forget now. A lot depends on this lunch.'

More than you know I thought. Whether my ex-wife's solicitor gets his caviare, for one.

'Here they are!'

'They' were Christie, her husband Max Mallowan, her daughter Rosalind and her son-in-law, Anthony Hicks. The vetting party – and we were four to two on the short side.

So this was Agatha Christie. A kind of benevolent, spreading Auntie. She seemed to me. But like the whatever it was in whoever it was's poem . . . she was 'something more'.

Luncheon was got through. I never saw a woman eat more, nor enjoy it more. She ate the equivalent of Saunders' share and my share twice over. Mind you, we neither of us did well. (I think I did not too badly as a matter of fact. In those days I tended to make much of provided food. But I didn't make as much as I could've and should've.)

The chat went round.

At one moment I resented my presence. Quite suddenly. 'You've worked bloody hard,' I said to myself, shooting a bit of melon neatly onto my knee, 'for sixteen years – allowing four out for Hitler – to get somewhere in the theatre. With some success. And here you are . . . ,' I continued, easing it off my knee on to the floor . . . 'eager to make an impression on an overfed, smug lady who needs you more than you need her. Or at least, as much as . . . '

Another bit of melon I managed to shoot on to Saunders' knee, which wasn't easy. Then I reflected that the lady was not only wider but older, considerably, than I. And, grandfather's whiskers or no, had made her mark on the world. Had comforted folk by the million. Especially those travelling by train. I waxed benevolent and actually ate a bit of melon.

The conversation had moved to *Black Coffee*. Not the liquid, the play which had saved Saunders' bacon. Up I came with a lie. I had never seen the play but I chirruped . . . 'Mrs Christie, I think I preferred the book!'

There was a silence you could have flipped a whole melon through chunk by chunk. Auntie actually stopped eating.

'It never was a book,' she said.

Saunders was pretending he didn't know me. Max Mallowan that he didn't know Mrs C. (Nor even Mrs M.) Rosalind began to laugh and Saunders followed suit. Christie was eating again. Rosalind's laughter I didn't object to. She may have thought it would cover the moment for me. Saunders was playing along, I didn't object to his laughter either. It was mirthless. I think. But when Auntie began to shake over her chicken or whatever to the extent of getting into a choking fit I went red and not entirely with embarrassment.

'I thought . . . ' I fumbled . . . . '*The Murder of Roger Ackroyd* . . . I thought it came from that . . . . '

'No, it didn't,' said Christie distinctly, jaws champing again.

'Oh,' I said. Rosalind continued to laugh. Mallowan and the son-in-law (had they read it?) joined in and Saunders made four. The rest of the luncheon was, I was sure, a dead loss. They laughed a great deal at my expense but I was left with the thought that I hadn't given pleasure. I did – foolishly – mention something about coffee at the Ackroyds' but Christie (she may have forgotten the story) wouldn't be drawn.

I must interpolate here that I am not a person who cannot be laughed at. With humour. I can see the funny side of me with the best of them. Once, when Saunders and I and a third friend travelled to Sicily for a much-needed break in the routine, merriment was made of my toting an umbrella. I took it in very good part. Especially upon our arrival in Paris where we switched aeroplanes. The rain was hissing down. There was a three hundred yard walk from the plane to cover. I put up my gamp and marched off, leaving Saunders and friend to lump it – I took that very well.

The Hollow was mentioned. And I prepared to lay my second egg. 'I don't think,' I said, still groping for composure, 'there should be any worry about my both directing and playing.' Christie was working her way through a mound of ice-cream. Having eaten me whole I didn't think she'd still be hungry. She stopped in mid-spoon.

'Playing?' she asked.

'Shit!' I thought.

'Cristow,' I said.

I had let my boss down with a bump you could have heard in the Haymarket. He came in with some very tactful remarks and the moment had a Band-Aid stuck over it. 'Only if Mrs Christie approves,' was his drift. I felt like a schoolboy having his exercise corrected. I didn't like the feeling one little bit.

I had begun rewriting. No permission had yet been given but it would be, said Saunders.

'As soon as Christie gets to know what you're doing she's bound to see it's for the best.'

I wasn't as sure. 'The first act,' I said to Saunders, 'is a series of dialogues.'

(A lot of people would say 'dualogues' but I don't care. I have always been fussy about words. I enjoy words, I may say I love them. Over the last twenty years our language has fallen to ruin like the face of Ronald Colman's beloved when it meets the outside world in *Lost Horizon*. Colman was devastated and so am I. But we peg on until we peg out.) I continued:

'Two characters we don't yet know discussing people we haven't even met.'

'Cut,' said Saunders.

'I have,' I said. 'To the bone. If I cut any more the characters who have gone to dress for dinner won't have time to do it before they come on again.'

'Do what?'

'Dress.'

'We'll have a quick-change room.'

'But . . . ' I explained . . . 'it isn't enough for an actress to strip off her day things and leap into her evenings, the audience must accept that she has had time to change at something approaching her leisure. It's *theatrical* time I'm concerned with. She would take a hour, I'll settle for ten minutes. Not . . . ' I added firmly ' . . . three.'

We didn't want to pad, this would have been a disaster, we compromised at about six.

We agreed between us that Jeanne de Casalis should be given her comedy head. Her Mrs Feather personality could prove to be invaluable. She was all too willing. At the end of Act One Christie had a stage full of characters trooping off to dinner in silence. This, of course, is reader material, not stuff for an audience. You can't sit and wait. So I penned two pages of 'overlap' dialogue. That is to say, the characters – six of them – move off to dine chatting as they go. No one line of dialogue is intended to be distinguished.

'All I want to hear,' I said to the cast, 'is a murmur of casual conversation. I just don't want you all to slope off as though you'd been struck dumb.'

I wrote these lines with care. The characters spoke, as it were, in character. Veronica, the film star, had made an exit as dramatic as her entrance. Clearly, they would discuss her. People not in the entertainment professions would regard such a celebrity as someone with two heads. (Such a bi-capital character as Veronica might well seem to the Angkatells to have four.) I gave to Lady A. a line to suggest that she had seen Veronica in a film and was confusing her with Dorothy Lamour who, if you remember, wore a sarong quite often. She would also confuse 'sarong'. My line ran: 'I've seen that girl on the films. She wore a sari . . . very low cut.' Jeanne added a gesture to indicate that the lady was ahead of time and appeared – to use the later, strange expression – topless. This scored a laugh which made the matter difficult. After the chatty general exit Henrietta was supposed to turn at the door. I, as Cristow, was on the terrace looking offstage after Veronica. The dialogue ran:

HENRIETTA: Coming, John?
JOHN: What? Oh, yes. Yes, of course.

(Brisk exit) CURTAIN

Now, this laugh achieved by Lady A. spoiled the moment. My Stage Manager put me wise about the 'topless' gesture. I took it up with my leading lady.

'But, darling . . . ' she said – she always began 'But, darling . . . ' – 'It's a funny line.'

'Not very,' I said. 'Not as I wrote it. In any case, I don't want to hear it. Not wait for it, I mean. Not laugh at it.'

She fixed me with a Gorgon stare. 'You're the director,' she said. 'You write me a funny line and you ask me not to get a laugh? To make it inaudible?'

Put like that it was a potent argument. She lost it.

Jeanne's ability – indeed, craving – to wring every ounce of comedy from her character was something we would need sorely to pull that first act out of the mud. Later in the play she had a line that should have run: 'Beautiful fresh eggs. They were laid this morning.' Jeanne adjusted this to run: 'I laid them myself this morning.'

I considered. Lady A. might well come out with such a confusion. There was no drama around at the moment to spoil. I let it go. I suppose I was vindicated when Lord Mountbatten nearly fell out of his seat laughing.

We thought about a setting. Christie had given us more problems here than the script had red herrings. We needed a terrace with windows opening on to it. Important. It was up on to this that Cristow was to step to get his comeuppance. He looks off to Stage Left, sees the murderer, utters a word or two of recognition and says 'Put that down' (the revolver). It doesn't do him any good. He gets one in the stomach or thereabouts (we didn't use blood or anything like that, we'd have gone through shirts at a rate of knots and economy was the keynote) and staggers down into the room to curl up and die Left of sofa.

We needed a French window downstage Right. (If the New Wave had broken at the time we opened some critics would have had a field-day. Anything, you recall, during the modern theatre renaissance, that smacked of a French window in something that smacked of a play was a red rag – or, if you consider politically, a blue rag – to a very raunchy bull. We had two. French windows. But the year was 1951; Ken Tynan hadn't yet said the word.)

We needed a fireplace, a door. We also needed – and this drove us nearly into the ground – a 'breakfast nook' (sic). Christie further described this as 'a curtained recess in which a piece of statuary can be supposed to stand, though not visible to the audience'. Cristow, at one point, goes into this recess to have a butcher's at Henrietta's work. He comments on it. Ergo, the breakfast nook can't be just tucked away somewhere, it has to have pride of placing. Yet – when this butcher's and chat are done with the nook is no longer needed. It must not, ergo, distract by the importance of its position.

Joan Jefferson Farjeon, the designer, managed very well indeed. She gave us, in effect, a recessed addition to the room. The entry to it was through an arch and a curtain hung to one side of this. I was able to have it closed when necessary. When it was open the distraction was minimal since I arranged for it to be minimally 'dressed'.

Furniture. I chose the pieces with care after trips to here, there and Hammersmith. A small escritoire Down Right, a Sheraton table Up Right Centre to hold drinking stuff, a low coffee table. A wing chair. A pouffe; I felt this room would have one. And a sofa. I made a deal with my boss. I had the perfect sofa in store at my flat. It needed covering, that's why I wasn't using it. The present material was brocatelle but my daughter, when small, had bored a hole in the arm with her finger and begun examining the stuffing.

'If,' I said, 'you cover it at your expense I'll lend it to you for the run.'

This sofa was well used during the action of the play – eight times a week for a year. By the time I got it back it needed covering again. But I was happy to have lost out on this particular deal. I used it again in a later production for another management, stipulating this time that if the play ran for more than three months it would be re-covered for me at the end of the run. This was inviting the worst, I realised too late. The play didn't even get to London. Today, the sofa – many times re-covered – is retired and lives in Portugal.

Came the day when Christie was to attend rehearsal for the first time. Saunders knew and I knew that this was so that she might vet me as an actor. As a director I had been accepted. Saunders had mooted 'certain little easings in the writing . . . which, of course, if she didn't like . . . ' It was the dual role that was in question. Christie – I think –had the suspicion Saunders was saving money. Which, of course, he was. But he wouldn't have offered me the two jobs had there been, in his view, a danger of putting the production in jeopardy. I trusted him but Christie didn't. As yet.

Like rain to spoil a cricket match Christie had kept off for a day or two. We had been hard at it and I knew my lines – very few of them Christie's. My character had to enter and be irritable and blather on about all the places he'd rather be than spending the weekend at The Hollow. (Perhaps he had a premonition he was going to get his comeuppance in Act Two, Scene One.) He went on and on – and on – about the South of France. Ah, the mimosa, and the rest of it. I'm not kidding you, this Dr Cristow went on and on about this mimosa. Now, I can take mimosa or leave it. I wouldn't say I'm a 'man with soul so dead who never to himself hath said' and all that. I can even take in other people's native lands. But this mimosa . . . I said to myself, I said, when rehearsing in my sparsely furnished flat (my ex-wife had all the good pieces, except for the sofa with a hole in the arm) . . .

'Get into the character,' I said. 'He doesn't necessarily think as you do but you're an actor, act! This Cristow,' I said to myself, 'is kinky for mimosa . . . '

And so on. But I did rewrite. That bit. I had rewritten quite a lot of bits when the time came for Christie to vet me.

'Give her Act One,' said Saunders.

Presumably he wanted her to see what I had done to make her dialogue digestible by watchers and hearers rather than readers. We did our nuts. Christie sat there like a large bird uncertain whether to lay an egg. I just prayed we wouldn't. I sat beside her and Saunders sat beside me. He'd been, at one time, a professional poker player; you never knew what cards he held. I was thinking of my ex-wife's solicitor. And watching and listening as director of the whodunit. I was young and able to do all three.

Came the moment for me to step in as actor. As I rose, I thought 'Sod this' and this, I think, gave me courage. I sailed through old Cristow's first bit and came back to sit beside Christie rather like a high jumper who has made it over the bar and returns, flushed, for a pat on the back at the bench. I got it. I was surprised as hell. Said Christie – in a whisper I don't think she meant the cast to hear – 'I shall be very sorry when you're dead, my lad.' The line has, of course, to be considered in context.

Saunders and I were spending a great deal of time together. We shared a feeling of complete disregard for the hands of a clock. I would work into the small hours and continue going at *The Hollow* until they became quite large. And I knew that, in his abode, he was worrying the night away. He lived in Edgware Road, I in George Street, three minutes distant. Often I would pop over to him for scrambled eggs, his culinary speciality. As often he would telephone me late at night and pop round to my habitat for nocturnal words. We talked of the past, the present, the future. We talked of plays, we talked of women. We talked of words and music, of Hutch, of Harry Roy (Saunders had been his press agent). We examined the world and pulled it about like monkeys searching for fleas. I remember these night sessions with enormous affection.

On one occasion – we were driving round Hyde Park Corner at the time – he said suddenly:

'Why don't you come in with me?'

He had no partner – not in the active sense. He was a man of integrity and of considerable business acumen. I had thought of a possible link-up of our interests. I could offer experience in the practical side of theatre. I was creative, perhaps intuitive. It might have worked to both our advantages. If 'advantage' allows of putting money in second place. (Back to Cockie!) It could be that Saunders would never be happy to do this. It could be that I would never be happy to see it placed first. This could have made for a perfectly balanced partnership. It could also have made for one in which the scales toppled over at the eagerness on either side to shove weights on the what'sits.

'Well?' he pursued.

Every instinct told me that this was a first-class proposition. 'I'd like to,' I said. 'But . . . no . . . thank you.'

The truth of the matter was that I would have staked my last penny on the idea. It was gilt-edged. What I couldn't tell Saunders, have never told a soul until now was that I had already staked my last penny. On a marriage.

CHAPTER FIVE

Thunder and Lightning

Tactful re-shaping of a denouement . . . How to wear tails when not playing Emily Bronte's dog . . . Throwing light on murder – and off it! . . . Strangulation at the Stage Golfing Society . . . I win a pound from Christie and she pays up . . . A storm about thunder and lightning and more 'Hollow' laughter.

I was still working like an unpaid fiend on the text of *The Hollow*. I must tell you at this point that, having directed *Potter's Notch*, a charming, beautifully constructed American play, I wasn't all that strung up about my first West End work in this field being on a whodunit. It was a challenge, I'll say that for it. Over and above the normal directorial chores – or should I say 'under and beneath'? – you have to keep constantly in mind the need for guiding the detective thinking of the audience. Actors must behave in character but they must also be given things to do which delude the audience. Its attention must be diverted suddenly to what must appear to be a significant clue – and, just as firmly, it must be diverted away from a truth. Sometimes you take a wild and dangerous chance. You attract its notice to a truth – hoping that the force with which you do this will convince them it is a lie.

'Mrs Christie . . . ' I said one day – it wasn't yet 'Agatha' and 'Hubert', this came slowly – 'I've been thinking about your denouement . . . '

'What about it?' she asked.

She wasn't too defensive. She was a shrewd lady and had come, I think, to recognise that I knew a few of my theatrical onions. I had made vast changes already and she made fewer and fewer protests at each. (The need for tact all the way was a very tiring factor, I decided, in this first production.)

'It takes place in daylight,' I said.

'Certainly,' she said. 'It's the afternoon.'

'More effective if it happened in artificial light,' I said.

'Yes,' she said, a little reluctantly. 'For the stage, perhaps that's true . . . '

It was the first intimation she had given me that she was thinking in terms of theatre. Up to now I had had the impression the book was the thing.

'. . . but it's the afternoon, so it can't and that's that.'

I smiled like a conjuror who knew he already had a bird concealed in the lady's bust-bodice. I had burned many a quart of midnight oil over this whodunit. The third act peak of a *play* is one matter. There is such a thing as a 'build' in writing, a peroration in performance. With a whodunit the whole evening is leading up to, 'You want to know who shot him? I did!' – or very nearly words to that effect. This, blurted out while the sun shines in, it occurred to me, would be milk and water. In nice, artificial, pooly lighting it might be made to have the kick of a slash of the hard stuff.

'There's a way,' I said and left the thought hanging. She began to get cross.

'I don't see . . . ' she huffed.

'This house in this play,' I said, 'is called The Hollow. It is set among trees and what not . . . '

'That's right,' said Christie.

'It would take little more than an overcast sky to make 'em turn on the lights. Yes?'

'Yes,' she said.

'Henrietta and Gerda arrive from the inquest – by the French windows,' I said. (Damned near everybody entered by the French windows in this play, you couldn't do a thing about that. I don't know why they bothered to have a butler, he didn't even do it!) 'Suppose,' I went on, 'we have a darkened sky and a couple of lines of dialogue like . . . ' (I had already written them) "We've beaten the storm. Good heavens, it's as dark as night in here!" . . . and Henrietta switches on a lamp?'

Now this, though I say it as should, was to make the whole difference to the denouement in *The Hollow*. I was sure Christie would go over the wall with delight. She didn't even raise an eyebrow about this bird I had made fly out of her top. She merely concurred.

'All right,' I said. 'Now we have another problem.'

'Oh?'

'Gerda is near to hysteria. Henrietta gets her settled on the sofa. "Gudgeon won't be back from the inquest," she says.' (Gudgeon is the butler who didn't do it and hardly ever shows anybody in.) ' "I'll put a kettle on and make you a cup of tea".'

'Yes?' said Christie.

'Well . . . ' I said. 'Your stage direction reads '*Exit* HENRIETTA. *Enter* HENRIETTA. HENRIETTA: "The kettle's boiling, tea won't be a moment".'

'Well?'

'Takes a bit of time to boil a kettle,' I said patiently.

'What do you suggest?'

I had hoped she'd make a suggestion for once – especially since it was getting through to her that this novel was now going to walk and talk.

'I have an idea,' I said. 'I'm not mad about it but it's the best I can come up with.'

She didn't speak and I didn't like the look of her at all.

'A mere touch of lightning . . . ' I said, ' . . . followed by a faint rumble of thunder . . . '

She was in like a dinner. 'I hate thunder and lightning in my plays,' she said with what I can only describe as pleasure.

I didn't go for this. 'I couldn't agree more,' I said. 'It's rather painting the lily . . . ' (I didn't see why I shouldn't allow myself a little pleasure.) 'I'm not mad about the idea, I mentioned that I wasn't. But it achieves two things.'

'What things?'

'Firstly, I don't like mentioning a storm as a trick to switch on. In this way we do follow through. Also, if we have a reaction from Gerda . . . '

'What kind of reaction?'

'The kind any hysterical woman might give to a storm – and I stress it would be a distant one. I don't propose a firework display and a twenty-one gun salute – slight lightings-up of the sky, two in number, followed by slight murmurs . . . Where was I? . . . yes . . . If we have a reaction from Gerda – a slight one' (oh, my God!), 'we give Henrietta time to put the kettle on. And so forth.'

'We could try it.'

'What?'

'We could try it.'

'Oh. Oh! You like my idea for putting the denouement in artificial light . . . ?'

Styles. The house the Christies named after *'The Mysterious Affair At . . .'*. It was to have its own mysterious affair.

Agatha ('Teresa Neele') arriving at Leeds with her sister.

'If it's necessary.'

'I think it is. Don't you?'

'We could try it.'

In the days of careful husbandry in play production the director planned his own lighting. I had begun planning mine, for *The Hollow*, while I was working on the dialogue.

Lighting can be of paramount importance to a stage production. In particular, to a thriller. If you're presenting a matinée al fresco the Almighty does the lighting and it is simple disaster. Better in the evening when He switches off and leaves it to the union members. I played several seasons at the Open Air Theatre, Regent's Park and the overall diffusion of daylight in the afternoons was death to everybody's concentration. It was damned difficult to keep the audience from nodding off. It was difficult to keep from nodding off ourselves. In *A Midsummer Night's Dream*, nodding off forms an important part of the action. Poor Fay Compton as Titania was hard put to it on her mossy bank – she and all four 'lovers' (I was, variously, Lysander and Demetrius) *had* to nod off. Our difficulty was waking up. At night, the difference was, in fact, electric. There is something about the playing of light on to a stage. But it should not be evident to the audience that a play is 'lit' at all. The general effect is all that need concern them.

I disapprove most strongly of the modern fashion for hanging the electrical ironmongery within view, anywhere and everywhere. The mystique has moved, it occurs to me. Lighting was formerly to dazzle the audience, to pull the magic wool over their eyes. Today, managers are dazzled by the manufacturers of lighting equipment into thinking so much of it is necessary. Perhaps the managers, in turn, feel that having paid the earth for it they should exhibit it? The audience, sitting expensively, should be assuaged by seeing just what it is getting over and above the actors and the play? (To follow through, of course, the manager should exhibit the technicians.)

Even in my early days as a director, it seemed ludicrous to me that a realiser of a play should also light the piece. A director might have been well grounded as an actor – most actors were well enough grounded in stage management. But to suggest that, because he makes not too bad a job of putting a drama on the stage, he is ipso facto the best person to paint it in its true, visual colours . . . is yet another example of theatrical lunacy. He is the cheapest, certainly. His down payment and his percentage were intended as an all-in cover. I travelled here, there and everywhere in search of furniture, props – even ladies' wear. The stage manager does some of the preparatory hunting but the final choice – and responsibility – rests with the director, God save the mark (or the pound sterling).

My grounding – on many a front – was pretty good. I was in the Birmingham Repertory Company as a lad. My first part was a lead in *Petticoat Influence* in which I wore tails for quite a bit of the time. I was a diplomat, I think. But most gentlemen characters got into evening gear, most real gentlemen dressed for dinner at home, wearing black ties. If they sallied forth to dance they put on a white tie – which meant a complete change of everything, trousers too. In the theatre, actors were expected to possess and wear on stage when necessary:

One dinner jacket and trousers,
One evening dress suit,
(Some actors used the same trousers but I was conscientious. Full evening dress required trousers with double braiding) . . .

To go with the above: Boiled shirts, stiff winged collars, studs . . . Black waistcoat for the dinner jacket, white for the tails. Socks, shoes. And, of course . . . ties. Double-ended. (And *never* made-up!)

The wearing of white tie and tails was second nature to us. Today, actors have untold trouble. The excellent television series about the Duke of Windsor had Marius Goring (an old hand) as King George V beautifully turned out – and wearing his clothes beautifully. It also had an actor whose good performance I was unable to assess in one sequence because his clothes were incorrectly worn. His white tie showed above the back of his coat collar and his white waistcoat below the cutaways of his jacket. Two cardinal sartorial sins in any wearer. And the character portrayed was by way of being a leader of fashion! In a recent, excellent again, production of *Private Lives* we had actors with their evening ties *beneath* the wings of their collars. And I am staggered at the number of actors who don't know how to tie a bow tie. Oh . . . In addition to the items marked above . . . We had to own and provide for wear on stage:

Two 'lounge' suits,
One sports jacket and flannel trousers . . .

Shirts, ties, socks, shoes to go with the above.

We paid for our own laundry (quite an item when you consider boiled shirts and starched collars – and waistcoats, the laundries did these beautifully). Anything out of the ordinary like a dressing gown or jodhpurs – or safari clothes if you were depicting Stanley looking for Livingstone – was provided by the management. The ladies too. (Their clothes.)

In my second play at Birmingham I stage managed and played Emily Bronte's dog offstage. I barked quite effectively – yelped too and whimpered when Emily beat me – through a lamp-glass.

We young actors went through the full rough-and-tumble. But I never got into electrics. I think I did pull the odd switch from time to time (today this would cause an immediate strike) but I didn't know what the switch was doing or why. Stage management – and the acting of roles from diplomat to Mr Badger in *Toad of Toad Hall*, from Hamlet to the Gardener in *Figaro* (yes, the opera) were a good preparation for being a director insofar as realising a play might go. How do you gain lighting experience? (We didn't think we'd need it in any event, our futures would follow a simple pattern, we would become great stars in the course of time and other people would light for us.) We did get it, unconsciously, by watching the effects achieved by our directors, by falling over floods when they were used at ground level and by being 'on' when lighting changes took place. And by reading a bit. It wasn't that satisfactory. Today, sensibly if expensively, the director confers with a lighting expert and they exchange ideas about what is wanted and how best to achieve it economically. (In the case of the non-commercial theatre, of course, economy doesn't get a look-in.)

Lighting equipment was vastly different. Not so much the equipment itself, though that has changed, as the availability – the willingness of a producer to come across with it.

Formerly, a commercial manager would rent a theatre with such lighting as it already had. He wouldn't want to hire extra lamps from an outside firm unless you, the director, said they were vital. If you did, he would choose the moment to decide whether or not you were vital. The normal equipment already installed in a straight theatre might consist of:

12 spots on the front bar;

a 'number one baton' (a line of smaller lamps) a little farther up-stage;

footlights – or 'floats' (so called because they were once wicks floating in oil) – with three or four circuits . . .

(Floats have disappeared, bringing the actor into your lap. Whether you as an audience want him there is another matter. I've always felt it to be best that a magician – and actors are magicians, no more – should keep his distance. I don't want to see the rabbits hidden in his hat before he produces them.)

Over and above this illumination you would find:

A few – 8, 10, a dozen? – F.O.H. (Front of House) spots pointing from the Dress or Upper Circle;
a few – 3 or 4 – floods (large, square, 'flooding' lamps) in the wings;
with luck, perches – spots mounted on stands at the sides of the stage;
the odd 'acting area' mounted on the spot bar (each covering a widish area with overhead light) . . . And – hurrah! . . .
a couple of door strips.

These were strips of wood to which were attached half a dozen or so ordinary bulbs. You hung them near a door, offstage, so that a character making an exit from a lit setting didn't look as though he was walking into a closet.

Without boring you – or myself, for that matter – I venture to mention again that, broadly, my theory of lighting is that, like make-up, it should be unnoticeable. (In some modern musical productions it is *intended* to be noticeable as a necessary adjunct to – or replacement for – the talents of those being lit. I speak of the fairly normal play.) Theatre lighting should enhance the picture without the likelihood of a spectator observing: 'How the lighting enhances the picture!'

Your first hurdle is the shadows. Shadows are normal enough, you have to have them, they follow you about. On a stage, they may distract. Even old Hamlet will be hard put to it to hold his audience if his every gesture is being enlarged in shadow form on what we thought was an Elsinore night sky. You have to preserve the balance by playing light not only on Hamlet but on the sky. Not too much or you won't listen to Hamlet. Not too little – shadows again.

An acting area lamp, shining down on you, will cast minimal shadow. (The shadow, such as it is, will be on the floor.) It will also – as every woman knows – make a ten-year-old look like a bloodhound who has been out on the tiles. Lighting, to flatter – or even to help rather than hinder an appearance – must come from some other direction than above. From a side, from below. (In the film studios many a lady is happy if the lighting cameraman gives her a 'pup' beneath the camera for a close-up. This small light plays on her face from well below chin level and a slack facial muscle doesn't stand a chance.)

Distraction, of course, outranks flattery or non-flattery. Take an interior scene. Play a light at an actor from the side and you get his shadow on the wall. Which is not – given real-life room lighting – where it would be. (Mind you . . . if a person were to lean over a table that bears a lamp, even to the point of his face being immediately above the light, you could frighten the daylights out of an audience. All right, it's a hammy trick but I didn't hesitate to use it later in *The Mousetrap*.)

Some lower their lighting to avoid shadows. (In days when floats were naked flames and mounted on a board, they were, literally, lowered by a rope to dim the lighting. Down went these floats through a hole in the floor at the front of the stage. It was a primitive form of dimming. Quite often, it set fire to the theatre.) Some reduce the illumination with 'artistic' intent. I remember Ivor Brown – a great critic – saying of a 'crafty' Old Vic *Hamlet* in the thirties: 'The production was played throughout in that near-darkness known today as "brilliant lighting-effects".'

The job, as I see it, is to keep the visual action flowing, aided and abetted by lighting, with no leaping shadows to take the eye. Nor even stationary shadows. When we moved *The Hollow* from the Fortune to the Ambassadors' I had hell's own labour keeping the shadows of the French windows off the foliage. Here's something strange. In real life, shadows from a well-lit room *would* fall on to nearby nature. There would be shadows on the foliage. In the theatre our view is too concentrated, the shadows are not acceptable and therefore distract.

I well remember this lighting session at the Ambassadors'. No time at all it would be done in, I told the manager. Wasn't it a simple matter of repeating my Fortune Theatre lighting? Theatres differ.

At the Ambassadors', because of the shallowness of the stage, the cloth was that much nearer to the window. Shadows, like Orlando's verses, on every tree. I managed it. (I had to.) We took a break – an expensive one, the electricians were on double time – and went up the road. When we came back I was able to breeze it but it isn't an experience I am proud to recall.

A final word on lighting. Years later I was present at a production of *Romeo and Juliet* at the refurbished Old Vic. It was no longer the penny-pinching Vic of Lillian Bayliss, it was now state-supported. (It never needed to be in Lillian's day, she would have been surprised at the change. She would have welcomed it, of course, money coming in was always fine. She just wouldn't have liked dishing it out to the actors. She once engaged me for five pounds, then tried to get away with paying me four.) There were, hanging about the auditorium, some hundred or two spotlights. These played upon the actors from more angles than Euclid knew about. Nevertheless, when poor Juliet came to her potion scene – which is pretty important – whichever way she turned she was in shadow. I reflected, not too modestly, that I could have served her better with 12 on the bar, plus FOH and perches. You wouldn't have seen them, either. You'd have given Juliet Montague your undivided attention.

We rehearsed *The Hollow* in strange places. Acceptably strange in those times. Theatres were expensive and not often available. We did our early work in rehearsal rooms, hoping to get into a theatre for, say, the last week. Normally, a play – unless the Arts Council of Great Britain is footing a large lump of the bill – rehearses for three or four weeks. We were shuttled back and forth, to and from pubs, church halls – the Young Women's Christian Association off Tottenham Court Road . . . I think it was upstairs at the Stage Golfing Society that I gave a talking-to to my cast about this 'delude the audience' caper. In fact, it was quite fun to do. It had little in common with direction as such, it was Hampton Court Maze stuff.

I put in a couple of cigarette lighter clicks. During the questioning by the Detective Inspector of the assembled country house party he makes some remark or other about a possible culprit doing this or that . . . As he pauses to take a breath a character he has his back to lights a cigarette. Nothing more, no emphasis. Merely the click and the flame. Only one other character – by the turn of a head – takes any notice. The Inspector continues. But the attention of the audience has moved for a moment to the character who is now smoking. At another point the Inspector is questioning one member of the party. Another member, immediately at his back, is nervously searching in her bag for a cigarette. She finds one and puts it to her lips. She is about to search again, for a lighter. The Inspector, without turning to her, takes out his own lighter, clicks it alight, then turns to put it to her cigarette. In each of these cases no double motivation needs to be given to the actor. In the first instance he merely feels the need for a cigarette and takes one. The effect on us as an audience, however, is quite different. In the case of the Inspector, he – as a character – is directed to be conscious of nervous movement behind him. A slight inclination of the head and he realises what the movement is about. To the audience . . . the fussing character is drawn into the puzzle. Just that, no more.

An instance of double motivation is as follows. The afternoon at the Stage Golfing Society was devoted to the denouement. In the moments leading up to it I had Henrietta move behind Gerda who was seated on the sofa. Gerda – wife of the murdered man – was slumped forward and snivelling. The solution of the mystery, we had learned, depended on the whereabouts of a certain revolver holster. I said to Henrietta . . . 'I want you to lean over the back of the sofa, put your hands on Gerda's shoulders and draw her to an upright position. Then move your hands forwards and backwards again on her shoulders and near to her neck. At this point your character is the one most under suspicion. Old Cristow ditched you, you have a motive. You're a strong girl, a sculptress, we can imagine you giving him one in the belly. This weakling wife of his might be able to blow some sort of gaff. I want the audience to feel you are about to squeeze what life there may be in her . . . out. The reason you – as an actress – must give yourself for these hand movements is a simple desire to give Gerda strength – you want her to brace herself.'

It worked a treat. Just as we, the audience, thought Gerda was going to get hers, Henrietta came out with the line . . . very quietly . . . 'There's just one thing Gerda . . . what did you do with the holster?'

An intake of breath from the audience on the first night told us we were home and dry.

We were forever fiddling with the text, trying to take it off the written page, where it was doggedly at home, and make it come alive. At one rehearsal – in a theatre, with Christie spreading over a seat in the stalls and me walking up and down the centre aisle – my ear was drawn to the Detective Inspector. The word 'peremptory' came into a speech of his. I can't think how I had come to leave it there. But what disturbed me more was his mispronunciation of the word. He wasn't to blame, the word is hardly ever given its correct sound. He plumped for the general mis-stressing of the second syllable. (Today after little more than a quarter of a century the correct pronunciation, as I was brought up to know it, has disappeared from most dictionaries.)

'It isn't "per*emp*tory",' I said, 'it's "*per*emptory".' The cast all turned in surprise to look at me. So did Christie.

'It isn't, you know,' she said.

'It is, you know,' I said. 'Look it up.'

'Bet you a pound,' she said.

'Done!' said I.

The actor made another stab at the word, getting it right for me but wrong for everyone else.

The following day, Christie inserted herself into her accustomed seat and I began my perambulation as this same scene was played. I was standing beside her – not coincidentally – when the actor came to his verbal Becher's Brook. He sailed over it and turned to me with a 'How's that?' expression on his face. Christie was handing me a pound note. I took it. But, at the same time, I called out to the actor . . .

'Change the word.' (With a side glance at Christie.) 'I don't think this detective would use it anyway, make it . . . "short".'

'Why?' asked Christie.

By now she was ceasing to object to changes. This question was merely a request for information.

'Apart from anything else,' I said, 'if you and I had a difference of opinion about the pronunciation to the extent of risking a pound on it, the word may fuss an audience. In my view they'll be more fussed if he says it my way because they'll think he's wrong. If he says it your way – which, mainly, will be their way – they'll think he's right but the odd philologist in the audience will know he's wrong and will be fussed. Then there's the point that a detective – this kind of detective, even if he used the word probably wouldn't get it right anyway. Now. For whom is he to make it wrong – you or me?'

'Have a peppermint,' said Christie.

There were moments when I almost warmed to her.

When I reported to my boss that I had won a quid from Christie he went white.

'You . . . didn't take it?' he murmured.

'I most certainly did,' I said. 'Nothing stand-offish about me. Do you think she wouldn't have taken my quid if she'd won?'

'But I know you,' he said. 'You were betting on a certainty.'

'I always do. I can't afford to lose. She can, though. What's more, watching us rehearse she's learning lessons no money could buy.'

We came to the Dress Rehearsal. It took place in a theatre. I don't remember which. We were to tour the play to get it further into shape but this was a preview for the management. And the author.

We reached the denouement. I had given direction that what used to be called 'lightning sticks' – something to do with magnesium, don't ask me, I burn myself lighting a candle – should be employed. Just twice. From the audience's point of view this was the most subtle effect. Barely noticeable. The kind of lighting-up-the-sky that might – in a summer storm – evoke the remark: 'That was lightning, wasn't it?' Each flash (very minor, the word didn't express it) was followed by 'my' thunder. No thunder sheets (steel carpet hung up in the air backstage and rattled. These had served for others. For me, they always sounded like steel carpet hung up in the air backstage and rattled). My thunder was achieved rather in the manner of the eighteenth century actor/author/manager at Drury Lane. You don't know the story? He wrote and played in a play that flopped. It included an invention by him of stage thunder. Cannon balls rolled along a wooden trough. He was cross when his play folded and attended the first night of the play that followed in. They had thunder and they used his idea – possibly his trough and balls, left behind. He strode up and down at the back of the auditorium declaring, in not too quiet a voice: 'By Heaven they've stolen my thunder!' He gave, at least, a metaphor to the language. Where was I? My thunder. Same principle. I got the ASM (Assistant Stage Manager) to roll a round counterweight (the cake-shaped metal things that hold the scenery up) down the stage. Most stages have 'rakes' (are sloped) and you just pushed the counterweight gently and it rolled like a wheel on the wooden stage making thunder. Of course you have to be careful to keep up with the thing. On one occasion, later, it did get out of hand and went on rolling until it hit the wall of the Prompt Corner. No such misfiring tonight. The thunder roared as gently as any sucking dove, as old Bottom had it.

At this preview Christie sat well in evidence. (An author should be invisible to actors at all times; they find their presence inhibiting. So do directors.) The lightning sticks lightened. My ASM thundered distantly, I even wondered whether she was too distant. It was a honey of a zephyr of a storm. You could have shoved it in a teacup. Christie called out (this is something else playwrights don't do) from her seat.

'I still don't like the thunder and lightning.'

I considered she had let me down. With, so to speak, a bang. I had discussed it with her and consent had been given. Now, in performance, if she didn't like it, thought we had been wrong, had decided it was her job to come up with an idea covering the interval needed for Henrietta's tea-making – well and good. She could have made a discreet note and told me afterwards. She chose to bawl me out in front of the assembled cast.

Discipline in a theatrical company is no less than that needed in a military ditto. You don't, if you're a captain, have your colonel bawling you out in front of officers and men. No colonel would be such a fool. Mind you, in a military case no man would dare to react. In my theatrical case my co-star – a lieutenant, say – began to titter. NCOs and other ranks (parts big to small) took their cue from Jeanne De C. I think I came nearer to walking out of that bloody production at that moment . . . Why didn't the management say something – had it gone home? I stepped from the wings – where I had been hovering over that thunder like a buzzard (if it had gone wrong I'd have eaten the ASM alive) – on to the stage.

'Mrs Christie . . . ' I said.

I was surprised at the amount of ice in my voice. (My ex-wife's solicitor, prepare to tremble.) I noticed that every titter had been silenced.

'If you can think of a better fill-in for the time it takes Henrietta to boil a kettle and make a cup of tea I'll be delighted. But, as your director, I must tell you that "I'll put the kettle on for tea", exit Henrietta, enter Henrietta, "The kettle's boiling" won't do. It might sell on a bookstall but it won't work in the theatre.'

There was a silence deader than Cristow. It occurred to me that Saunders might be in the lavatory having a go at shooting himself with Gerda's revolver. I turned the knife.

'If you like I'll give the company a break while you rewrite the scene?'

'No,' she said. 'I think it's all right. Let's leave it.'

Ever so slightly vindicated I continued with the rehearsal. I never, though, did feel the same about my fellow actors after that titter.

CHAPTER SIX
Smash Hit

How not to get a laugh – even from an undergraduate . . . Blood and Debussy . . . Christie drops me a couple of pages from Baghdad . . . I have two sleepless nights and move into a movie . . . The tide I didn't 'take at the flood' moves on to Fortune . . . Director or magician, it works! . . . Smash hit.

We opened at the Arts Theatre Cambridge. During term, but the age-twelve laughter of the age-eighteen undergraduates was, in fact, a help. Saunders came back to my digs for the autopsy.

'There was a laugh,' he said. 'When Gerda was being questioned.'

'I noticed it,' I said. 'It won't be there tomorrow.' Gerda, Cristow's mousey, hysterical wife (how did he come to marry her? But you mustn't worry about details like that.) had to say 'John was cross with me on the drive down. I change gear so badly.' Not an inspired bit of writing. And Joan Newell, excellent actress, had got an unwanted laugh.

'How?' asked Saunders.

I had directed only three other plays. A beautiful American piece which I loved, a rare costume high comedy, and a not very good farce which I had had to doctor heavily. I had doctored *The Hollow* heavily but it was my first experience with a whodunit and lessons had to be learnt.

I had had pretty extensive experience, as an actor, in playing comedy. Any comedian will tell you that the sure way of losing a laugh is to break the sentence, you have to get the line smartly away to leg.

For example:

Ex-wife's solicitor: I expect this bill settled by Friday.
Ex-husband: What about Saturday?
E.W.S.: I won't be here on Saturday.
E.H.: I'll look in on Saturday.

If E.H.'s reply is delivered as:

I'll . . . look in . . . on Saturday.

he won't stand an earthly. If he's expecting a laugh. I decided to apply this in reverse.

'You'll see,' I said to Saunders. 'I've called a rehearsal for ten-thirty tomorrow morning. The laugh will be out.'

I explained my theory to Joan Newell who reacted to it like a true professional. I got her to say:

'I change . . . (pause) . . . gear so badly . . . '

That night, not a sound. Pin-drop stuff.

There was one more unwanted laugh to be eliminated. By a method less subtle. Simple excision.

Sometimes, the nearer you get to a thing the less distinctly you are able to see it. Once, as a child – very nearly, I had the ambition to become a doctor. I decided I didn't like blood. I prefer it contained in vessels and veins and running smoothly.

'Nearly everyone,' said a doctor to me in later years, 'has the same squeamish worry. Medical students faint in droves at operations.'

'Suppose the surgeon faints?' I asked.

'Don't think that has been known. The secret – I find – is to get in there up to your elbows in blood and guts. Then you don't see it as an outsider.'

This, in directing *The Hollow*, was what I had done. Got in there up to my elbows in Mrs Christie's blood and guts. So close was I to it that I missed this one point by a mile. We all did. Not a one of us saw this coming, not even A.C. It was, in particular, my job to see it so I carry an unforgettable can.

Edward and Midge, his diminutive cousin, meet at this Hollow weekend after a gap in time. She has grown up in the interim but he, older in years, continues to regard her as a child. She has always loved Edward and tries to jolly him into looking at her as having taken puberty in her horsey stride. She curls up at his feet (or it might have been on that pouffe. I can't remember where I put her; I know she was looking up at Edward. Higher than just normally 'up' I mean) and the dialogue ran:

EDWARD: You haven't changed.

MIDGE: How do you know, you never look at me. I'm a woman, Edward!

EDWARD: I wish I saw more of you, Midge.

Whether it was that the actor and actress in question played these lines with such sincerity at rehearsal that they became acceptable, whether my humour was such that I didn't look with undergraduate eyes for dirt in everything . . . or whether – as aforesaid – I was too near the bleeding body . . . I let this pass though, as I write the lines now, the funny side sticks out far enough. At that opening night in Cambridge poor old Edward brought the house down. It was as though Max Miller had hit the University town. Atmosphere so lost is not easily regained. At the following day's rehearsal I had Edward substitute a tender look for the offending line and, for the rest of the week, the theatre adolescents were deprived of a leer.

We had many failures at this try-out. One was pointed out to us by the local newspaper. They referred to 'glutinous film music'. And they were bang on the nail. I kicked myself. At one stage, again, the action had been expected by the writing to stop cold. Edward leaves the room and returns with a revolver. Now, it takes a bit of time to hoof it as far as the gun room, pick a revolver and return. Moreover, having returned, he sits down and writes a letter. Not so much a letter, more a suicide note. I've never – up to this date – written one but I imagine it would take the odd couple of minutes. All right, as with the changing for dinner in Act One I would settle for 'theatrical time'. What is the shortest such a note could be? 'Shooting self, Edward'? I thought the moment needed helping. I resorted to the device of having Midge, a little earlier, switch on a radio. Music came out of it and overlapped into Edward's scene. The music saved our Christie bacon. Edward could have had time to shove 'To whom it may concern' at the head of the sheet and tell them how to dispose of the remains. Only one thing. It was the wrong music.

'It's a melodrama!' I said to myself as I kicked. 'You don't need melodramatic music! Something simple. To play against the mood of the scene.'

I substituted Debussy's 'La Fille Aux Cheveux De Lin'. The difference was unbelievable, it was just the job. (I also cut out the suicide note for insurance.)

Agatha's comments came to me from the Middle East:

British School of Archaeology
Karradet Mariam
Feb 19th Baghdad

Dear Hubert,

I have now heard from several friends who saw the show in Cambridge and where several opinions coincide, I think it might be well to pass them on to you. I'm dealing only with the adverse criticisms, and, on the whole, enthusiasm has predominated but we don't need to bother with the bouquets!

To deal with the smaller points first: The acting as a whole was not up to the standard of Lady A. This I think is not true, but is due to over brilliance on Jeanne's part. I am quite sure that the cast as a whole is good.

Several objections to the 'farce' in Gerda's performance (but some liked it). This, I think, we agree should *not* be. Also a criticism of Edward as being too much a 'figure of fun' throughout. Possibly this also has been remedied.

Everyone liked Midge, Gudgeon, and the Inspector and thought they couldn't be better, and that Veronica was exactly what she ought to be and 'probably was a more important item in the whole than one realised'.

Sir Henry 'not very convincing'.

The maid 'did a good job'.

Henrietta seems to have been found disappointing, though her looks made amends, but didn't quite get across as the woman she was meant to be. However, since they were all biased by having read the book, I don't think this is a fair criticism. Half the book is devoted to 'building up' Henrietta.

Top marks – Lady A. (Superb etc), the Inspector and Gudgeon.

Now to the one criticism which worries me – since it deals actually with the play and is, I think, justified.

This is, that the Edward and Midge sequences are all crowded together, huddled in a bunch. (a) Edward changes from Henrietta to Midge. (b) Midge gets it wrong. (c) Edward tries suicide, all one after the other, crowded into about ten minutes.

I did feel this myself a little during rehearsal – but hoped it was all right really and that no one would notice it – and anyway I couldn't see how to obviate it.

I'd like to know what you think about it – and if it *is* actually bad theatre. I've thought of a possible rearrangement of the third act. It's a bit difficult, because I haven't got the script out here – but on a separate page I'm sending you a tentative reconstruction to see what you think. It would, I suppose, be possible to try it out before opening in London. I'll have to leave it, I think, entirely up to you. If you're satisfied with the sequence the way it is, then leave it.

Excuse the awful typing. I've only got a very peculiar old machine out here and it does funny things.

I haven't had my daughter's devastating criticisms yet – if you see her, you will probably get the brunt of them! If she tells you the show is really quite good, remember that will be extravagant praise!

How I wish I could see the play. Why will nobody ever put a play of mine on in the early autumn?

Yours sincerely,

[Signed Agatha Mallowan]

Agatha's 'separate page' ran:

POSSIBLE ALTERATIONS IN ACT III

Opening: the same with the detectives arriving. Gudgeon possibly says he is not sure if Sir Henry is in, but will search for him.

Inspector then goes to verandah centre, speaks to Sergeant about exactly where Cristow was standing when shot etc.

Serg. And Edward Ankatell was in the woods, so he *says*.

Midge's entrance with suitcase and scene with Inspector. Ends with her telephoning to shop while detectives go out centre pursuing their researches.

Midge gets through to the shop straightaway and Edward enters R. whilst she is telephoning and their scene proceeds to engagement, being finally interrupted by return of Inspector and Sergeant from verandah.

Natural embarrassment on part of Edward and Midge. They may or may not say they are engaged, but they go off together R. Midge saying, 'We *must* find Lucy and tell her.'

Agatha—as I remember her.

ARTS THEATRE, Cambridge

Managing Director: Norman Higgins, M.B.E.

MONDAY, 5th FEBRUARY, 1951 **For Six Days**

NIGHTLY at 8-0 **Matinees : Thursday and Saturday at 2-30**

ALL SEATS BOOKABLE IN ADVANCE : 7/6, 6/-, 4/-, 3/-. Monday Eve. and Thurs. Mat : 6/-, 4/-, 3/-, 2/-
Box Office (Telephone 2000) Open Daily : 10-30 a.m. to 8 p.m.

PETER SAUNDERS presents

JEANNE DE CASALIS **HUBERT GREGG**

in

The Hollow

THE NEW PLAY by

AGATHA CHRISTIE

with

BRYAN COLEMAN

JEN WRIGHT

NIGEL FITZGERALD

JOAN NEWELL

DIANNE FOSTER

A. J. BROWN

PATRICIA JONES

MARTIN WYLDECK

RICHARD SHAW TAYLOR

and

BERYL BAXTER

Directed by Hubert Gregg

Decor by Joan Jefferson Farjeon

PRIOR TO WEST END PRESENTATION

The original billing for *The Hollow.* It was becoming the fashion for managements to have their billing matter expressly designed. An expensive business and not for new, struggling producers. The words 'The Hollow', from a special block, were all that could be managed on our budget.

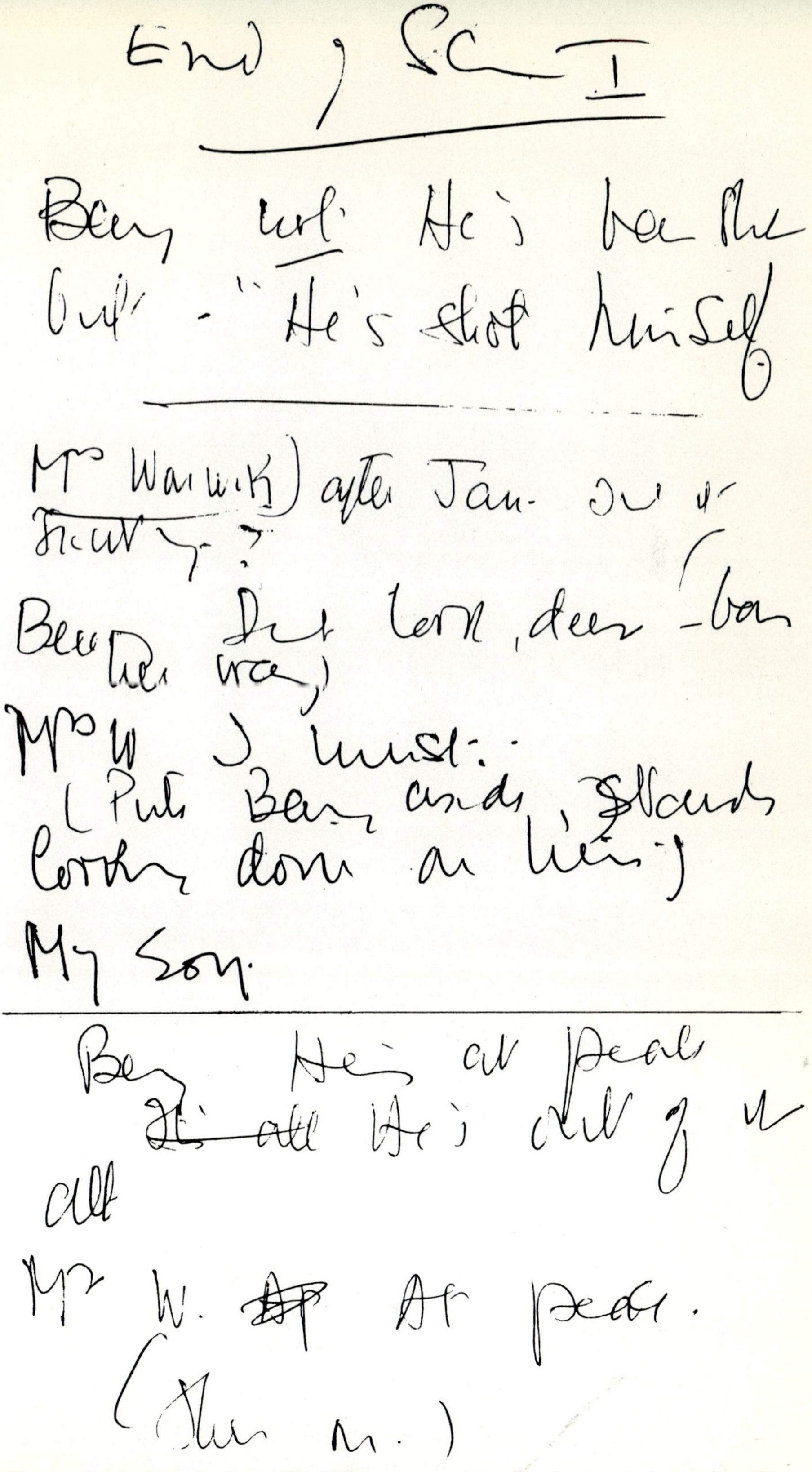
End of Scene I

Benny (wild) He's been the Only — "He's shot himself."

Mrs Warwick) after Jan – Out of Sanity –?

Benny Don't look, dear – (bars her way)

Mrs W I must:
(Puts Benny aside, stands looking down on him)

My son.

Benny He's at peace. ~~It's~~ all He's out of it all

Mrs W. ~~At~~ At peace.
(Then in.)

The typed help I received over *The Hollow* was one thing, handwritten help another. The above relates to *The Unexpected Guest*.

Prince John dressed to kill. (The author in the film part he left *The Hollow* to play. It was in this gear the publicity department wanted me to appear on television singing 'Maybe It's Because I'm A Londoner'. Normally I'm easy-going, in this case I put my mediaeval foot down.)

Peter Finch and the author in the Walt Disney movie *Robin Hood*. Note the backcloth—and the stonework.

Sergeant then says: So it was *her* he was keen on and not the other one.

Inspector: So it seems.

Then either (a) Doris and her scene, followed when she runs off by entrance of Sir Henry

or (b) Sir Henry, and scene with Doris takes place when he goes to check up on revolver.

Then straight on through Gudgeon, Lady A. etc.

Lady A goes off R with remark about man run over by tram and immediately after Edward and Midge come in centre and tell Sir Henry the news whereupon he immediately goes R and calls Lucy back:

Sir H: Lucy. Lucy, come and listen to this.

Scene between Lady A, Midge and Edward as before. Sir H. assists but does not participate except for one or two short comments 'Of course' when Lady A says be married here, and 'Really, my dear' when Lady A expresses hope band of trousers will not be too tight.

Scene ends with Henry looking at watch, time to start, are you ready, Lucy? Where's Henrietta? etc. Arrangement as to cars. Lady A. goes off L. Edward to get out his car.

Midge left with Sir Henry has the little scene 'Is it really all right?' Henrietta etc.

After which I think it is all plain sailing to end.

During this prior-to-London tour of *The Hollow* I was asked to make a screen test for the part of Prince John in Walt Disney's *Robin Hood*. I shot up to London, tested and was offered the part. At this period I was doing quite a bit of filming and it seemed a chance not to be missed. 'There is a tide in the affairs of men' and all that. I had told Saunders about the test. What he thought about the likelihood of my getting the part I don't know but I didn't think I stood an earthly. Actors were being tested in droves. They narrowed it down to Geoffrey Keen, Kenneth More and me and the director, Ken Annakin, apparently considered I was the rightest to play this villainous creep.

I got the offer and the problem. It would mean re-casting Cristow – though, presumably, I would still be able to find time to direct another actor as the Gloomy Doctor. *Robin Hood* was to be a major movie so there would be weeks of preparation, costume fittings and so forth before we went on the floor. We had decided we must make certain other cast changes in *The Hollow* so, in any event, there would be full rehearsals and another try-out before Christie would mystify the metropolis. Contractually I was free to accept the film but this was neither here nor there. Saunders and I were on a friendly footing and had there been a question of my leaving him in the lurch I would certainly not opt out because of a lack of words on paper. Equally, he would not have held me to a contract which would prevent me from taking this 'tide' at the flood and all the rest of it. Was it, in fact, such a tide?

Saunders couldn't have been kinder. He wrote me two long and objective letters setting out in 1, 2, 3 form the advantages and disadvantages of the two Johns, Plantaganet and Cristow.

I spent two sleepless nights – one for each letter – boiling it all down. I had never, in the first place, wanted to play Cristow. A star character who gets bumped off halfway through the play. They talked about him of course. They never stopped talking about him, listing all his bad points, but this didn't alter the fact that there he was, this sexy mimosa-kink, cold in the local morgue and going green. Mind you . . . the theatre was and is my first, as they say, love. My preference, though, is for a play. And I do like filming. I was waiting for some kind of a break in pictures and Prince John – for Disney – could be this.

Over my cornflakes on the morning of the second day I decided to leave *The Hollow* which, after all, would still be my baby as far as the directing went . . . and film for Disney. The movie, as it turned out, didn't blaze any trails but on balance it was the right decision. Not coincidentally, it paid off all my debts at one fell what'sit.

We managed to persuade Ernest Clark to play Cristow. He accepted when I showed him the changes I had made in the script as presented to him. He added a few excellent adjustments of his own. In the end he gave a careful performance many rungs above the play.

The London first night of *The Hollow* was to take place at the Fortune Theatre. Saunders had broken the news to me while I was still playing Cristow on the earlier tour.

'I've taken the Fortune,' he said. 'What do you think?'

He's out of his mind, was my first reaction. The Fortune is – or was – one of those theatres nobody can find. In fact it isn't far from Drury Lane stage door but try telling that to a tourist. It was the tourists Saunders was thinking of. Shrewdly, he had figured that, in Festival of Britain year, they might be tripping back from the South Bank over Waterloo Bridge – and find their way to Christie at the Fortune. Nearer than Shaftesbury Avenue, you had to admit. If the customers *can* light on it, the Fortune is a pleasant enough theatre. It was a gamble. And it paid off in spades.

The first act – as I have mentioned – was our worry. The second act would top it, we knew, and the third act would top the second. I had cut the first to ribbons and fiddled with it till the remainder fabric was all but shredding. All that chat about characters you hadn't met and folk leaving the room and belting back in their black ties and long gowns. We had the fastest dressing country house party . . . It must have been disturbing to walk the halls and stairways. Ladies haring about, zipping as they went.

But we had Jeanne de Casalis. She had driven us Harpic, as the phrase of the day went (clean round the bend), throughout rehearsals and both tours but now we were to assess . . . well . . . her tour de force.

I sat in the front row of the Dress Circle. We knew, Saunders and I, that if the audience went out half happy to their first interval drinks, we were away.

Jeanne gave her Mrs Feather act as we had never had it before. Laughter – not hilarious but chuckly and persisting – floated us through that difficult act like the developer over a slowly appearing photograph. The babble of conversation as the assembly left the room for dinner . . . I had drilled them in this new dialogue like a platoon, even Jeanne let that laugh line carry her off without a stop.

'Coming, John?'
'What? Oh, yes. Yes . . . '

and his brisk exit with Henrietta. A curtain beautifully timed by the stage management. And we held our breath. Applause – not deafening but full and happy – broke out. The audience, as it rose to leave for the bars, gave an almost audible sigh of contentment. I had a brand new date for the evening and jolly attractive it was too. I grabbed it by the arm.

'I need a drink,' I said selfishly.

And that wasn't all.

We took our seats for the second act.

Cristow got his wee note from Veronica, screwed it up testily and chucked it at the waste paper basket. (Later in the run the stage management forgot to 'set' this disposal prop. Halfway through the scene a hand appeared from the OP (Opposite Prompt) side with a wastepaper basket in it. I wondered what the Christie fans might make of this strange manoeuvre.) The doctor died a treat, doing a beautiful touch-down at just the right spot. Not easy. It was a small stage and when the house party milled on to have a look we didn't want anyone to trip over the body and go a purler. Nobody did. The second scene opened and before you could say 'Where's the butler?' we were into the question and answer bit. Nobody coughed.

It was thrilling for me to see all my little ploys – the whodunit tricks that had nothing whatever to do with directing in the real sense – pulling their weight. It was a different pride, though, from the glow I had felt at the reception of *Potter's Notch*. If I was preening the odd feather this night it was as a magician rather than as a realiser of a play.

GERDA (to Inspector): 'Who could have wanted to kill John . . . ?' (Who not?) A moment's silence . . . the scratch of a match and Sir Henry lights his pipe. Only Lady A. looks at him.

The two lighter clicks. Two small murmurs from the audience, one at each. Nary an unwanted laugh. I correct that – one. Unwanted – it seemed – only by me. Lady A. proffers a box of chocolates to the Inspector. He declines.

'Soft centres,' she tempts. Adding, 'There's a jelly baby . . . '

'No,' I said to Saunders when he suggested the line. He took the matter, on appeal as it were, to Jeanne de C. She put the line in and brought the house down with it.

'There you are!' said Saunders.

'I'm not,' I said. 'I still say you don't have jelly babies in a box of chocolates.' (Strangely, today I believe they do make up the kind of mixture that might include what might be termed a jelly baby. Hardly the stuff for Lady A. Again, today it might be.)

'It gets a good laugh,' said Saunders.

'Don't we all?' I said.

Edward sized up his Midge, undressing her with a gentle look instead of words. He went over big. Later, the peace of the Debussy was a perfect musical foil for the turmoil in Edward's mind. We didn't need him to write that won't-be-seeing-you note.

Came the denouement. It worked like a bracelet full of charms. Down went the lighting . . . just two notches and carefully timed by the stage management. On came Henrietta and Gerda . . .

'We've beaten the storm . . . it's as dark as night in here . . . '

Up came the pool of artificial light as planned and Henrietta made her beeline for the kitchen and the Earl Grey. A barely noticeable moment of sheet lightning. Gerda reacted her stuff. As she reached the terrace door . . . an almost imperceptible rumble from that counterweight. Thunder – was it?, we wondered. Yes, we thought. Gerda nervous but containing it all . . . She is drawn to the spot where Cristow had lain dead. Then to the sofa to sit centre of it. The sobs begin. Enter Henrietta. Then to the hands on the shoulders, the bracing . . .

'What did you do with the holster?'

That glorious gasp from the house . . .

Following a denouement it must be free-wheeling downhill at speed. Bring the wee play to its curtain. The Inspector gives Gerda the drink she has poisoned for Henrietta and there we are. (What is going to happen to him when he puts in his report God alone knows. Or cares.) Down comes the curtain and the applause bursts like a storm you don't have to hold in. It goes on and on.

Away I went with my date to Ciro's and a good time was had quite extensively. Next morning the notices were excellent.

'The audience cheered another top-level mystery,' one critic wrote, ' . . . that rarity, a thriller about reasonable and interesting people . . . ' (I wouldn't entirely go along with the first adjective!) . . . 'intelligently and credibly acted . . . ' (It was, too) . . . 'A fascinating and intriguing exhibition of sleight-of-hand' said another. 'Not only one of the best play-puzzles London has seen for years but a thriller well laced with laughs which plays fair with the audience right to the end . . . '

This had been our object, to play up the comedy and play down the blood. He was anaemic, this Dr Cristow. I directed myself and

Ernest Clark to clutch hard and hidingly at the stomach. Today, of course, you'd be up to the gusset in gore.

'The answer is baffling,' said a third . . . 'It's ideal entertainment and, in fact, an enormous success which I heartily recommend.'

When a critic says that a whodunit is 'intelligently and credibly acted', this is a pat on the back not only for the players but for the management and, modestly I suggest, for the director who cast them. We chose after exhaustive discussion and consideration. With the production shaping up so well on the first tour we made changes. Sometimes expensive changes. Like a football club investing in the odd transfer in the hope he'll take them to Wembley. And bring them back with the cup. We hated having to make these changes. Certain members of the cast hadn't, we decided, quite the guns for London. Sheer lack of West End experience is something you can do nothing about in the short term.

('West End' have become two dirty words. Your modern Equity member will say that acting is acting, what is so special about London? I'll tell him. Style. Style isn't something that went out with Jack Buchanan. You can play a part in a sweat shirt and jeans and have style. Style – unlike star quality (two more dirty words) – is not, I think, something you have to be born with. It can be the patina on the leather after years of careful nurture. Leather cannot acquire this patina unless it is good leather to begin with but it isn't born with a patina.

We needed every help we could get with this Christie piece. We needed, for London I decided, actors with a potential beyond the quality of the writing. Actors who could show us that not only was this a good 'play-puzzle', the puzzle could be skilfully and attractively presented with all the multiple techniques at their command. If the vehicle was no more than a comfortable family jalopy it could arrive in the capital looking like – and running as smoothly as – a Rolls Royce.)

If you bring, say, a young actress into London before she is ready for the arc-light examination that 'West End' means, you could do her a disservice that would delay her eventual 'arrival' for two or three years. In discussion, of course, you don't think quite along these lines. 'So-and-so isn't up to it,' you say. 'We'll have to get a replacement.' Ruthless it sounds, and is. The redeeming point is that one kid's misery is the joy of another who gets chosen.

Through those French windows – and the door – at The Hollow passed some very good players indeed – and I include the ones who were not asked to follow through to London. Joan Newell who played Gerda proved to be a top class emotional actress. We had been fellow committee members of the Repertory Players – a society that gave playwrights and players a chance to be assessed in London in single Sunday-night performances. Directors too, *Potter's Notch* had been one. Beryl Baxter played Henrietta. She had made a small name in films as a contract artist with the Rank Organisation. A good-looking girl, with a natural style. Not experienced in the theatre but with a beautiful, and beautifully audible, speaking voice.

In the theatre audibility is a fetish with me. Since the coming of television, clarity of direction – which may very well be three dirty words – has gone by the board. Actors who think they can flit from one to another medium with impunity and without effort of technique to redress the balance are flagrantly guilty. Sadly, too, because I suspect they get no jollying up by most directors. Like 'business', 'audibility' is something it isn't really done to mention. Not only are some in power not interested in whether the audience comes in, they don't give a damn whether they hear what they've paid for when they do. I saw an *As You Like It* in the late seventies . . . I don't care to hurt anybody but *As You Like It* is so frequently done (sic) that you won't easily identify the production I mention. It was important and heavily subsidised, I'll say that. When the Jacques stepped forward to deliver his Seven Ages of Man bit (face to the audience, he'd been directed to give it straight to us – a good idea and an actor's dream of a position), I sat back to enjoy. After the first pentameter I sat forward again, straining to hear. It was a wasted effort, I couldn't. From first to last, not a bloody word. I don't mean the odd missed phrase, I mean not a single word. Luckily I knew the piece by heart but I don't happen to feel that such foreknowledge should be expected of a seat-buyer. In fact, I think I was a guest but the point remains the same. I would like to think the reason all national companies spend half their time and our resources doing *As You Like It* is because they hope, one day, to get it right.

Jessica Spencer . . . experienced – London experienced – and stylish to a degree played Midge (and was to graduate – if that's the right word – to Miss Casewell in *The Mousetrap*). She replaced Jen Wright who had given a good performance but was too young, we had to admit, for the part.

Colin Douglas replaced Bryan Coleman, a good and experienced actor who had, strangely, a little too *much* polish for Edward. The character needed a tweedy rough edge which Colin was able to supply, with an equally good performance. A.J. Brown was a perfect Gudgeon – the butler who, though he didn't do it has, in common with all the guests and staff, to lead you up to believing he might've.

Patricia Jones played the remainder, visible staff – the maid. A beautiful wee performance from an attractive lass. She had a particularly interesting bosom which, it did occur to me, might take the minds of the males in the audience off the whodunitry (the things a director has to consider!). We decided, on balance, to let it ride.

Ernest Clark who succeeded me as Dr Cristow was polish itself until polished off (sorry).

(One problem I had come up against in playing Cristow. I passed it on to Ernest Clark. This is a matter not easy to believe, I had the utmost difficulty in convincing the management. When you execute a movement eight times a week – once nightly, two matinées – an incredible amount of wear may accrue. I'll give an example which may well be received with a gasp, if indeed received at all. I played in a Rattigan comedy called *While the Sun Shines*. In one scene three excited lads spend two minutes at most on their knees, shooting craps. We did a great deal of sliding about the carpeted floor. Our trouser knees took a hell of a beating. More surprising, the toe-caps of our leather footwear took a beating too. The lad playing the American – he got more excited than the Frenchman and me – wore a hole clean through each toe in the space of three months. Replacements became acceptable and regular. It was the same with Cristow's trousers. All down one side he got it. Just falling down dead. A good job that, in life – so to speak, we only do it once.)

Dianne Foster played Veronica, the film star, as to the manner born – to the extent of being whipped off to Hollywood later to be one.

Poor Dianne was made by us to go blonde, I can't think why. She had jet black hair which didn't take at all to the treatment. At last, she had to be given permission to remain brunette. She was going bald.

Martin Wyldeck – a very natural player – and Shaw Taylor spoke for the constabulary. Martin – as the Inspector – spoke at some considerable length. The thing about an Inspector is he thinks up the questions. He gives the lead in every burst of dialogue, he must have gone mad getting the part under his belt. I felt really sorry he had to make such an ass of himself in the end. (As the Inspector, I mean. Martin went on to heights.)

The major replacement was George Thorpe who came in as Sir Henry. George I had admired since seeing him a dozen years earlier in *Quiet Weekend*. He had a long and very distinguished career. We played together in 1946 in a play that didn't reach London, called *Strange As It May Seem*. A depressing experience. At one Sunday train call we looked for the company's reserved carriage. The railway had stuck labels on the windows that read: Strange as They May Seem. George's companionship made the tour possible, we became good friends.

George Thorpe brought to my notice a theatrical phenomenon. As a writer of songs, I had marvelled at the ability of Alan Breeze, Billy Cotton's singer. Offstage, Alan had a stammer that brought him to a halt at every other word. Then, he would walk on, go to the microphone and sail through Phil The Fluter's Ball without a hesitation. Now I came across this in straight theatre form. George Thorpe was in agony with fibrositis. He gritted his teeth as I held his jacket for him in the wings. The body movements he had to go through in order to put it on made the sweat stand out. Then he was able to walk on stage, perfectly relaxed and easy. During the action, he had to bend down and pick up a letter. Whoosh, down he went and whish, up again like a ten-year-old. We made our exit together and, once through the door into the wings, he'd double up. The pain would hit him like some devilish magic. No doctor has ever been able fully to explain this. It would seem that one hundred per cent concentration on something can remove all consciousness of pain. Where does the devilry begin and end, though? Could an actor make an entrance swinging a broken arm? (I'm sorry I began this, I'll move on.)

The part of the benign, gun-keeping husband in *The Hollow* fitted George like a Colonial white glove. We came to words only once. At a rehearsal at the Whitehall Theatre. George's forte was his 'throw-away' du Maurier style. He began to throw away to the extent of being inaudible. I was wandering about all over the theatre, my ears pricked – I always do at the later rehearsals.

'George,' I called out, 'I can't hear you!'

He went red. Then he drew himself up to his considerable full height. 'I have been heard,' he said (now quite audibly), 'in theatres all over the world . . . '

'That's it,' I interrupted. 'Great. I can hear you now!'

'You bastard,' he said and that was the end of that.

These were the players who, with my help, had pulled it off for the management – and the author. All that remained was the test of the Agatha Christie name as a theatre draw in the long term. She was to pass it with flying colours. *The Hollow* played to packed houses at the Fortune Theatre for several months, then transferred to the Ambassadors' Theatre where it continued to run for almost a year. Saunders had a smash hit on his hands. His shrewdness in choosing Christie as his pulling name, his courage in renting the Fortune Theatre had enabled him, at last, to lay a Royal Flush on the table. He began to shuffle for the next hand.

CHAPTER SEVEN

A Play Called 'The Mousetrap'

A film, a novel and a theatre hit – boom time!... Christie lets me off with a glass of sherry ... I am marked out for crucifixion in Soho ... A play called 'The Mousetrap' (Who gave you that name?) ... I am invited to direct it and don't do but do do ... 'Agatha' and 'Hubert'.

Once a play has opened in London the director's work is virtually over. He continues to keep a watching brief, dropping in nightly, say, for a week, weekly for a month or so – then merely from time to time. He may call rehearsals if he thinks it advisable. A plea from the management such as:

'Old So-and-So isn't half hamming it up in Act Two. Can you go in and have a butcher's?'

Or:

'Young Thingummy's got whooping cough. Caught it from one of her bloody kiddywinks, I told her to keep away from 'em but no. The understudy is as nervous as the Pope at a family-planning seminar. Can you pop in to rehearsal this afternoon and tell her she's marvellous? Don't lay it on too thick or she'll want more money'

is treated with respect. If your contractual presence isn't on demand elsewhere you hop in a taxi and don't even charge it. You may, on your regular visits, give the odd 'note' to a member of the cast.

'Watch that flood on the terrace. I could see your shadow five minutes before you made your entrance ... '

or:

'Why have you changed to wearing lighter socks, I couldn't take my eyes off them ... '

Generally it is the job of the stage management to notice these matters and to keep an eye on the production as a whole to see that it remains in the shape finally approved by the director. Moreover, they should be quite capable of 'putting in' an understudy. Most stage managers are budding directors in any case.

Our leading lady in *The Hollow* I didn't look forward to visiting. If I left too long a gap between calls she would say: 'Darling! You're neglecting us!' If I dropped in more frequently I would be greeted with: 'Darling! What are we doing wrong *now*!' But there was no questioning her value to the production. Her performance varied only in that she continued to squeeze the dialogue like a sponge for the smallest drip of a laugh that might be left therein.

I had made my *Robin Hood* film and was now feeling a little envious of the actor who had taken over from me as Cristow. When I reflected that he spent the second half of the evening in his dressing room the envy paled in colour but I do confess to a weakness for liking to be – from time to time – 'on'. Directing I enjoy every bit as much as playing but I don't care to do either one for very long to the exclusion of the other. I was fairly free, waiting for the picture to be released and rocket me to high filmic demand. So, when Queen Mary expressed a wish to see *The Hollow* and to meet the folk involved, I got out my best bib and tucker and had a haircut. I had been presented to the historic lady on two earlier occasions but theatre people are always suckers for a pat on the back and I looked forward enormously to the hat-trick, so I had this haircut. I needn't have bothered. When my boss drew up the list of those to be presented he left me out. Perhaps after all he hadn't forgiven me for getting out from under old Cristow.

I was able to be helpful about publicising the play. The Walt Disney press department was working at full pitch. My first novel, *April Gentleman*, had just been published and Robert Hale were doing me proud. Photographs were posed – on the Fortune Theatre stage – of me showing the actors what to do (and acting my socks off in the process). Articles appeared – always mentioning *The Hollow* at some length. Robert Hale even paid for an advertisement in the theatre programme.

In the light of these goings-on, I was still surprised when Saunders handed me the script of a new Christie whodunit and asked me to read it with a view to directing it. I took it home and finished it within the hour.

Three Blind Mice wasn't, strictly speaking, a new play. Not even a new whodunit. Christie purported to be a busy lady one way and another. Having married Max Mallowan, the archaeologist, she used – perhaps expectedly – to follow him around and help to classify the things he dug up.

Christie is quoted as saying once 'The good thing about being married to an archaeologist is that the older you get the more interested he becomes in you.'

It always sounded to me like a press agent's ploy. (I don't think she needed a press agent after that disappearance but one might have needed her and come up with a sample.) Christie rarely made a bright remark in conversation. In my hearing, anyway. I have heard a group of people rock with laughter at the end of one of her sentences but this is not to say she was witty. She was – from the point of view of public observation – a retiring creature. She hated making speeches or being photographed. Perhaps the spectre of that disappearance was attached to her like the shadow Wendy sewed on Peter Pan.

With a success like that of *The Hollow* most playwrights would have done twenty-four hour stints to produce a 'next man in'. Some might be tempted to disinter an old one, give it a chance to ride on the back of the first hit. Christie – as said – purported to be busy but I doubt if she really was. She could polish off a novel like clockwork.

'Not next week,' she said to me on one occasion when I had saved up to buy her a lunch to discuss something. 'I'm writing a book next week.'

As regards her archaeological chores I think her sorting of remains never really moved into the category of high-pressure tycoonery. Yet she was extraordinarily unavailable.

Cards would arrive from Baghdad. (On this visit she was sorting *and* writing a novel. About digging.) Letters from Swan Court in London . . . I did go here for discussion – two hours on the first occasion, on one glass of sherry and then . . .

'We have to dine so I'll say goodnight.'

I had missed mine. My girl had kissed me good luck and said: 'I won't keep dinner, Auntie is bound to feed you, it's the least she can do.' It was the most, it seemed, and she hadn't made it.

Letters from Wallingford in Berkshire. From her house on the Dart. Disarmingly bad typing when they were typed, with hand corrections in pencil. It occurred to me to buy her a typewriter ribbon but my girl thought no.

'She never gave you as much as a small gin and tonic,' she said. 'And Agatha Christie doesn't need a typewriter ribbon. Let the reader puzzle it out.'

I seem to have wandered away from this new script. (One did so with ease, I was to find.) This *Three Blind Mice*. It seemed Christie – not writing plays at present and having nothing else in the drawer – had remembered an old something she had tapped out for radio. Queen Mary had asked to hear a Christie and Christie had obliged. Royalty to royalty. Now, Christie had tapped a bit more here and a bit more there and put it into something like theatre form. Not much but something. It was, at any rate, an easier exercise than adapting *The Hollow* from the book. She had shoved it into Saunders' hand and had gone off digging again.

Saunders and I knew Dan Sutherland at that time. We met every Saturday in Soho for lunch and discussion. Dan named us 'God the Father, God the Son and God the Holy Ghost'. Dan was God the Father, I the Son (clearly, it must have been thought, heading for crucifixion). Dan was a promising playwright. Saunders had presented, with some success, a play of his called *Breach of Marriage*. Dan was a great theatre-lover and a careful, hard working draughtsman with a typewriter and paper. And cigarettes on tap. I directed, for a Sunday try-out, a play by him called *The Fifty Mark*, an excellent comedy. No one bought it for the London stage but it was performed again and again on television. When I took this new Christie script I thought of Dan and his care and his midnight oil and cigarettes.

'Consider,' I said to myself, 'an unknown playwright getting his work into its best form, typing it, re -typing it. Paying, even, to have it typed finally – maybe printed – by an agency . . . You may feel that to dolly up an idea you had for the wireless and barely pause to stick a cover on it before you high-tail it off to some old Pharoah's grave with the idea of disturbing his rest and putting his bits and pieces on file . . . ' But then it doesn't do to let your imagination flow. All you get is fun.

'Yes,' I said to Saunders the following day. 'It dates a bit . . . ' (This was already 1952 and I didn't feel we wanted to hear characters rabbiting on forever about ration books. We had 'em still but we were trying to ignore 'em. As a matter of fact, I had lost mine. I think I was using my girl's.) . . . 'but it isn't a bad little whodunit.'

Strangely, my opinion hasn't changed after the event. I still think it isn't that bad.

'Can't use the title though,' said Saunders.

Thank God, I thought.

'Why not?' I said.

'Emile Littler has a play called *Three Blind Mice*. We'll have to change it. Christie hasn't any ideas . . . '

Here we go again. I thought, but not seriously, of a possible parody of another twenties song. I didn't feel, though, it was the moment to suggest 'MOUSEY, WHO DID YOU KILL LAST NIGHT?'. Be helpful, your girl needs her rations. To feed you with if no more.

'You could,' I said, 'call it *The Mousetrap*. Copying old Hamlet.'

'Old who?'

'Hamlet. It's the name he gives *his* play. The one that shocks old Claudius out of his cups.'

Saunders was considering.

'*The Mousetrap* . . . ' he said, imagining the title on a bill. You also have to say it, gauge how easy it may be for a potential booker of a seat to get his tongue round it – on the telephone, for instance. Take the case of the American lady who, in later years, wanted to book for Tom Stoppard's piece based on the original author of *The Mousetrap* (Hamlet). She rang up and said:

'I want two stalls for that play . . . *Rosencrantz* . . . ' She paused. Then tried again:

'*Rosencrantz and* . . . '

'*Rosencrantz and Guildenstern are dead*' helped the box office man on the other end of the wire.

'Gee,' said the lady. 'I guess I'll have to see somep'n else.'

Saunders had cogitated.

'Sounds all right,' he said.

The Mousetrap it became.

(Agatha herself has recorded that the title was her son-in-law's idea. Great minds? It's possible. I can only say that since the middle sixties an appreciable part of my living has come from the wireless and from the freakish fact that I have something approaching total recall. Except about where I left my umbrella. The conversation recorded above took place under the canopy outside the Fortune

Theatre during a performance of *The Hollow*.)

This *Mousetrap* was to run longer than Hamlet's. In the case of the Prince of Denmark it was a one-night stand that led, in the end, to domestic massacre. In the case of Christie it led to domestic bliss, apparently ad infinitum – if money galore can buy that and go on buying it – for Mathew Prichard her grandson (to whom she gave the rights rather than shower the tax man, though it is rumoured he sold out), for P. Saunders and for all who were shrewd enough to put their pennies in his piggy bank. Saunders had a continuing loyalty to those who, in his early days, had been able, financially, to express faith in him. No matter in how modest a way they were always given – certainly for some years – the first opportunities to invest in a new venture.

STOP

Revelation Ahead

But back to this new venture, this whodunit with the Shakespeare title. The setting was very different from the timeless, problemless country house comfort of *The Hollow*. Georges Simenon who –much over and above *Maigret* – was quite something of a writer said:

'I detest Agatha Christie, she writes about rich people, castles and beautiful scenery. I tried to read one of her books once but I never made it to the end. It isn't literature, it's embroidery.'

Having read – or mis-read (or mis-remembered) – only *The Murder of Roger Ackroyd* myself, I am not in a strong position to comment. Certainly this *Mousetrap* wasn't about rich people. It was about desperate people putting on a good face in a seedy hotel where the central heating doesn't work and rationing plays havoc with the dinner menu. What's more they're snowed in. They're a motley bunch. A bigoted woman magistrate, a flashy black marketeering Italian – who flies half way up the fourth wall to convince us he is a suspect, a girlish man, a mannish girl . . . a Major who turns out to be a detective sent to keep an eye on things (like Homer, he nods and a murder happens within reaching distance) . . . the host and hostess who suspect one another at the drop of a poker . . . then this nutty lad who comes in out of the snow and announces himself as a Detective Sergeant. The real detective doesn't arrest him, doesn't even bat an official eyelid.

Walt Disney Productions took this picture. The author on the set of *The Hollow* at the Fortune Theatre, 'directing' (L to R) Dianne Foster, Beryl Baxter and Jessica Spencer. The picture was one of many taken to publicise the movie *Robin Hood* but *The Hollow* did well out of them and it didn't cost the management a bean.

Another of those publicity pictures. The author (waving arm) 'directing' *The Mousetrap* for the umpteenth time. The cast (six of them, L to R) Heather Stannard, Barry Shawzin, Mysie Montie, Arnold Diamond, Patrick Doonan and Geoffrey Adams.

TELEVISION may have given the cinema a thrashing. It has taken over theatre advertising without charge.

Last night Granada gave "Speaking of Murder," which opens to-night at the St. Martin's, a free, 15-minute plug which should keep it running for a year.

After three excerpts on "Chelsea at Eight," producer Hubert Gregg ensured that a potential audience of millions wants to know what happens next.

Maxine Audley revealed a diabolical plot to murder the wife of the man she loved by locking her in a sound-proof, air-tight safe.

She lured her victim to the trap. A woman's voice screamed. We saw a woman's hand stubbing out a cigarette.

Whose?

I'll have to buy a ticket for the St. Martin's in the end.

NEVILLE RANDALL

Exposure on television helped *The Mousetrap*—even the non-Christie *Speaking of Murder*. It was death to a musical smash hit called *Chrysanthemum*.

To help two newcomers to production I designed this billing for *Speaking of Murder* at the St. Martin's Theatre.

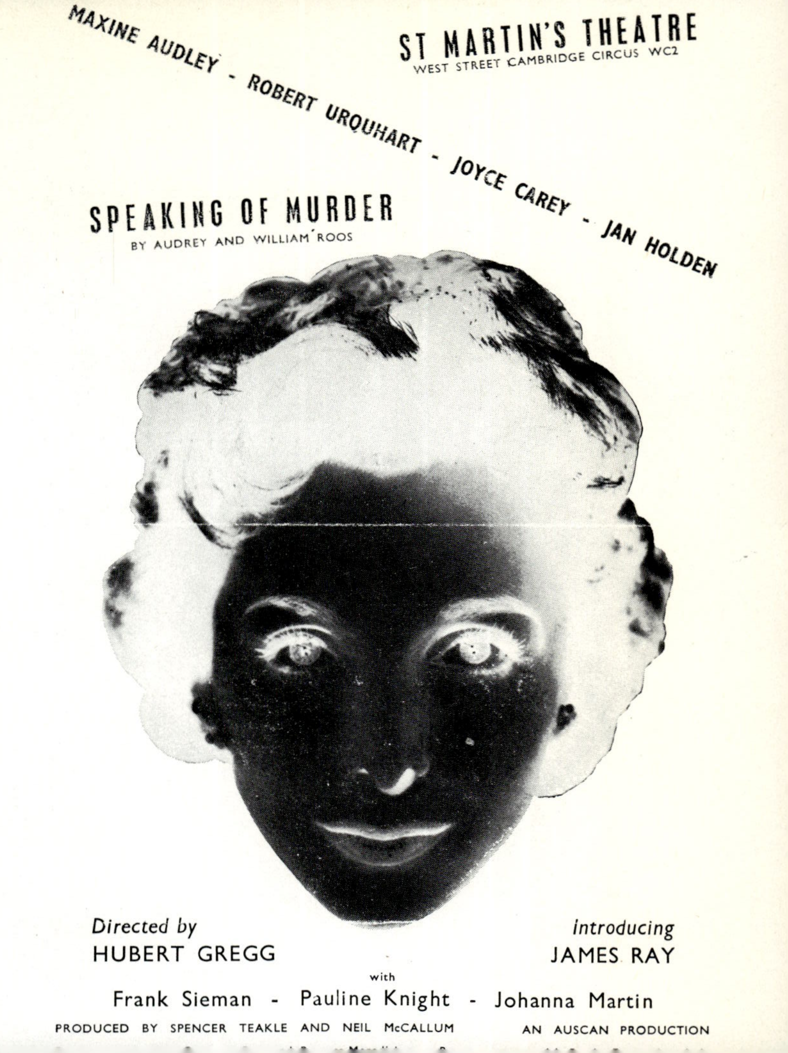

'You can't be a sergeant, you're too young,' says Mrs Boyle the magistrate.

A direct clue which nobody picks up since we have come to regard Mrs Boyle as a comic figure. Nothing she says will be acceptable at any level. A safe-as-houses character in whose mouth to put those revealing words.

Revelation Ends

Casting *The Mousetrap* was going to be a more than usually splitting Christie headache. Would she pull them in again, should we insure by getting the odd name in the cast?

I was working at the Garrick Theatre at this time. *To Dorothy – a Son* was a smash hit and Yolande Donlan was leaving to be replaced by Allyn McLerie. I was engaged to direct her in the new production.

'What about Attenborough?' Saunders asked me. (Dickie was starring in the play at the Garrick.) 'Do you think he'd be right?'

'Very,' I said. 'If he'll do it.'

'Put in a word,' said Saunders.

I was enjoying the directing of *To Dorothy* and was becoming very attached to the leading part in it. My feet were itching for the feel of a stage and it was an itch I wouldn't be able to resist scratching for long. But I was mindful of Saunders' embassage. One day, Dickie and I sat in the stalls during a break.

'I've been asked to direct the new Agatha Christie,' I said. 'You might like to play the lead in it. And there's a good part for Sheila.' (Sheila Sim – Mrs Attenborough.)

'Good,' said Dickie. 'Like to read it.'

'There's one snag,' I said, having been rehearsed by Saunders. 'It's being presented by an independent management. Chap called Saunders. He put on *The Hollow* . . . '

'Is that a snag?' asked Dickie.

'No,' I said. 'If it sounded like that Saunders didn't mean it – I mean I didn't . . . I mean he's all right. You'll like him.'

'What's the snag?'

'He's doing it at the Ambassadors', a small theatre. And we want as good a cast as we can get. The snag is how much you'll both want out of the kitty.'

Dickie considered. 'Let's read it,' he said. 'If necessary I'm sure Sheila would take a cut.'

In addition to presenting *The Mousetrap* Saunders decided to send out a tour of *To Dorothy – a Son.*

'Who's playing in it?' I asked. (There are only three characters worth mentioning – Toni, his wife and ex-wife.)

'I suppose you'd like to,' said Saunders. 'And direct it too, eh?'

'What's wrong with that?'

'Only one thing. You won't be able to direct *The Mousetrap* if you do, the two productions will overlap.'

'Mm,' I said.

The matter was mulled over and quite a bit of sleep was lost. But I elected to do *To Dorothy*. Christie wrote me the following note:

6th June, 1952

Dear Hubert,

Yes I am furious with you for not producing *The Mousetrap.* However, I do expect you will enjoy yourself in *To Dorothy A Son*. But think how annoying for me to have to get to know another producer. Anyway many thanks for having produced *The Hollow* so admirably.

Yours
[Signed] Agatha

Saunders too said he was sorry and was I sure and good luck.

The Mousetrap opened and the critics were kind. The cast was excellent. It was a jolly good little whodunit, no more, no less. And it looked set for a run. I was on the road having a ball with Roger MacDougall's marvellous comedy. (The scene in which Myrtle, the dumb-blonde American ex-wife is told she doesn't get the inheritance because of time difference around the globe is classic. Toni's explanation – as to a child – of this phenomenon makes up one of the funniest scenes ever presented on a stage. Finally, he mentions – casually – that, moreover, they crossed the dateline. 'What's the dateline?' asks Myrtle. Toni appeals to the deity with a look and the lesson begins again.)

The Mousetrap had been running for three weeks when, at Saunders' invitation, I went to see it. To give a free seat – I think I may even have got two – was so uncharacteristic of the management that I could not but feel something was in the wind. It was, I was to learn.

My reaction to the evening was as described above. At the final curtain a second mystery was unravelled for me in the auditorium. As Dickie stepped forward to make his speech a young man next to me sat bolt upright. He said to his friend 'Good Lord! That's Richard Attenborough!' Dickie had given an excellent performance, they all had. But attractive as some of these names were on the bill outside, it had to be admitted that audiences were more impressed by the lady who had disappeared when I was in knickers. Agatha Christie. The biggest name on the marquee.

Directors, if they bring home the ham, are in demand. Often they cross the Atlantic. Clearly, if they do they are not in a position to drop in on their London productions.My view has always been that a director's creative work – at rehearsals and up to the moment when the wheels are running well in London or New York or wherever – is what earns him his percentage. His stage director (now nominally graded as 'stage manager') should be capable of keeping the show up to scratch. If the director is in the right town and country and a problem arises he copes, naturally. But a manager should never, I feel, wish his director away from another production. The fact that his director *has* another production on hand is testimony to the manager's having made a good choice to begin with. *The Mousetrap*'s director, I believe, was unable to be 'on call' and the management – from its view, justly – was restive about this.

Saunders asked me whether I would take over. It was a friendly arrangement but I did insist on making quite a few changes. Anyone who has seen a Shakespeare play recently – particularly one financed to a large extent by the State – will appreciate that interpretation is strictly individual. I wanted my *Mousetrap* to have my cheese in it, at least.

I couldn't have been happier with the cast as chosen. One or two who should have been in their teens or barely out of them weren't but they were giving cracking performances. If they had been they very easily mightn't have, I reasoned. A new setting I asked for but didn't get. Understandably. I mentioned this annually for seven years, the understandability growing less with the flowing on of time and the flowing in of box-office receipts. (When at last I decided to withdraw from the production the new director was awarded a new set so I carried with me the feeling I had been helpful.)

'Monkswell Manor' is the name of the house in *The Mousetrap*. Saunders built a very nice house out of some of the proceeds and called it 'Monkswell'. I remember Jack Waller who produced the twenties musical whose hit song was 'Tea For Two'. When it was on the cards he would produce a musical I was to be in called *Chrysanthemum* (he died soon after the contracts were signed) he asked me down to Sussex for the week-end. 'It's easy to find,' he said, jotting down some notes. 'You turn right here, go on for a couple of miles, then turn left . . . At the end of the road, left again, then right . . . And you can't miss it, it's staring you in the face. A lovely little Tudor house called 'No No Nanette'.

'The Great Hall' at Monkswell Manor is the requisite Christie setting. As many entrances as you can cram in, suspects must be able to do the deed then leave in almost any direction. The Hollow – in the book – had a great deal of coming and going round a swimming pool. It was surrounded by a hedge with gaps in it, a sort of Hampton Court Maze with murder amongst the privet. On the stage we managed –how did we? – with two French windows and a door. This, though, when you analyse it, gives you five directional possibilities. The Great Hall at Monkswell gives you the same, now that I come to count . . . but it *appears* to have more let-outs than a colander. I don't know why. It always seemed to me, when I sat in the auditorium rehearsing, that anyone who booked in there as a guest must be an Eskimo, the draughts would come at you from every point of the compass. To say nothing of murderers.

The two young people who own the Manor (too grand a name, to go by the appearance of this room) are called 'Giles' and 'Molly'. Molly's aunt left her the place and they are going to try to run it as a guest house. This is their opening night and they're up to their eaves in snow. The central heating doesn't work and the coke hasn't arrived. (It wouldn't be much help if it did, would it?)

At the start of the story, Giles and Molly are both out, neither being aware that the other is, if you're with me. (This leads to suspicion the like of which you can't imagine. I always felt they needed not so much a delivery of coke as a Marriage Guidance Counsellor. But then, these hadn't been invented . . .)

The wireless tells us a murder has been committed in London.

(Somebody left it on, this is a good start for a guest house, they won't make a penny.) The voice of Frank Phillips – I think it's Frank Phillips, I haven't seen the piece for twenty years – gives us a description of the murderer that would fit anybody. (Except perhaps the touring midget who took over from me in *While the Sun Shines* when I was on holiday and left his bell-bottoms behind for me to wear. More of this later.) It fits, of course, to a T every member of this odd-ball house party. (A side thought: When *The Mousetrap* opened in 1952 wireless sets had valves. Even radios had them. It was a tiresome thing directors of plays had to allow for. You had to invent some visual interest to tide you over the ten seconds or so it took for the apparatus to warm up. Today the noise comes in at once. Unless, of course, your play is set in a pre-transistorised age. In which case the management had better send for me.)

Revelation Ahead

Soon, the Ralstons . . . that's the rest of their name, Giles and Molly . . . are receiving the weirdest set of Kooks since Handley. All right, the Goons. Three of them, anyway. A fourth is as dull as a thud, the fifth – murder material if ever you saw it . . . The last . . . this too young 'detective' of whom not even the real copper thinks to ask his credentials.

The murder takes place at the end of Act One. A good spot, they'll argue like mad over their miniatures in the bar. As in *The Hollow*, the victim looks offstage and mumbles a word that bespeaks recognition . . . The lights go out, the old bird gurgles . . . and the curtain falls.

Act Two and the questioning begins. Again, the suspects must have, each, two lines – directions, I mean – to follow. A reality line . . . and a 'red herring' line. The masculine girl – we learn in the mopping-up at the end – is the sister of the mad detective-murderer. In one scene, while he is 'questioning' her, she recognises him. Now, here is a yawning pitfall. The young man twiddles his hair, the sister thinks: 'My God, my brother!' We – the audience – must think merely that her fixed stare at him indicates . . . what? . . . a growing indignation at the questioning?

The actor playing Trotter has the mightiest problem of all. He must tell himself the whole pretence is a madman's game. He is playing at being a detective, relishing it, asking questions to which he knows the answers – or about whose answers he doesn't care . . . taking notes . . . An actor may be tempted, as the tension mounts, to display too clearly evidence of growing insanity. How far is the director to allow him to go? (Not as far as the author indicates, one of her stage directions has him 'reeling against the desk' in answer to a simple question. A reeling sergeant?)

The adroitness of Christie shows itself in the pace at which she is able to do the mopping-up. After the denouement, as I mentioned, it must be downhill all the way, no hold-ups. In a page and a half of dialogue – which we played, moreover at pace – she is able to unfold the following . . .

1. Mollie was Trotter's school teacher and let him down. This is why she was a near-victim.
2. The Major was a detective all the time.
3. Casewell was Trotter's sister. She warned the Major in the nick of. (Otherwise, would he have sat by while a second murder totted up?)
4. Paravicini was a black marketeer. We get his whole story in three lines.
5. Giles was in London to buy his wife an anniversary present.
6. Molly was in London to buy her husband an anniversary present.

Away with the mystery, in with the comedy . . . They unwrap the presents – her cigars for him (unsmokeable) . . . his hat for her (unwearable) . . . On comes Major Metcalfe who isn't (he's the detective, that's it) . . . At last he has detected something . . . But is he, as once before, too late? He can smell burning from the kitchen . . . Off goes Molly, holding on to her hat . . .

Revelation Ends

CHAPTER EIGHT

Don't Mention Money!

A diet of Bakewell tarts – Frank Sinatra – a midget leaves me his bell-bottoms . . . 'Don't mention money, we're subsidised' . . . Success can be murder . . . How to be happy in the long run . . . A song makes me independent . . . I enter the Central Criminal Court through a wall.

My name was, by reasons of contract, not allowed to be on the *Mousetrap* billing but this didn't worry me. I had, I think, put some sort of stamp on the production but there was that set. It was very good and all that but a director likes to have a say and I hadn't and I didn't see eye to eye with it at all.

Each November, now, the cast was changed and there were auditions and startings from scratch. It was hardish work – a bit like trying to whip up everlasting milk. Financially, it was not condignly rewarding. (Had it not been for careful – even rigid – budgeting all round in the first year or two *The Mousetrap* might have had merely a rattling good and not a world-shaking run.) So why – many have asked me – did I undertake it? I have asked myself. A sense of obligation? What obligation, to whom did *I* owe an obligation? Unquestionably the success of *The Hollow* had prepared the road for *The Mousetrap* and I had turned down the direction of it, initially, for my own indulgence. Perhaps I had a sense of following through?

A word about long runs. Quite a few words. Long runs are something about which, as an actor, I feel deeply. As a director, I know they mean a continuance of the need for checking care – and also of percentage. You don't have to attend the theatre eight times a week though, and tell the author's story from the beginning, if anyone has a beef the actor has. But beef is meat. It beats tea and cherry bakewell tarts which is what I had to live on when I was a juvenile. At the Aerated Bread Company in the Gloucester Road. Any run at all that came my way meant solid meals and a warm coat and a room you didn't have to sneak into when Mrs King wasn't looking. I mentioned *autre temps, autre moeurs* in another context. I mention it again in this.

Dry rot was discovered in the theatre in the forties. It was too late to call in Rentokil. When I left whatever it was I was in (well, they did shunt me about) I followed another actor into *While the Sun Shines*. (The play where we wore out our trouser-knees and toe-caps and had to have renewals.) It ran and ran, this play. So, of course did the war. (When it began some wag said about the war 'The cast is too big, I don't like the lighting and the costumes are terrible. It can't run.' It did. Not as long as *The Mousetrap* – it wasn't easy re-casting some of the leading parts – but it ran.) It just happened that *While the Sun Shines* was still running when the war closed. Every night before going to bed, as we listened to Frank Sinatra singing 'Nancy With The Laughing Face', we said a thank-you prayer to the God of Long Runs.

One night Hugh Wakefield knocked on my dressing room door. He had succeeded Ronald Squire as the Duke of Ayr and Sterling (the part I was to graduate to thirty years later. They asked me to direct a revival and suggested I might play the old fellow too. 'Bit of character work,' I thought to myself. 'Be fun.' Then I looked at the Duke's description in the printed copy and found Rattigan had put his age at four years younger than me.) Hughie looked ill. His face was white under his Five and Nine. (That's the stuff we used for making up our faces – Leichner sticks, Number Five, Number Nine. It cost ninepence a go now it's eighteen shillings.) 'What's the matter, Hughie?' I asked. (I knew he'd resigned from the Green Room Club. Because he couldn't get his horse in the lift, they reckoned.)

'They . . . they want us to take a holiday,' he stammered. 'I don't want a holiday, do you?'

'A what?' I said. I hadn't had a holiday since 1938. It appeared Binkie Beaumont, our manager, had conceived the idea of our taking a rest. Today, such luxuries are commonplace – it's all part of 'cradle-to-the-grave', you get paid for it. Binkie wasn't going to pay us.

We had won the war but they wouldn't let us leave the country. They may have been afraid we wouldn't bother to come back. I spent my unwanted, unpaid furlough in Bournemouth where I had first heard of Agatha Christie from the Gay Cadets. They weren't there any more. Bournemouth wasn't the same. You couldn't swim out, for one thing – not and hold on to your manhood – there were bloody great spikes sticking up out of the sea, put there to impale Germans. Then, the General Election happened while I was there. Having heard the result, I wondered whether it was worth while taking the Belle back to London. But I did have a job. That's what you kept telling yourself, you did have a job. It would never have occurred to an actor to entertain a crazy idea like *leaving* a *hit play*!

It breaks the rhythm. Stepping away from the eight-times-a-weekly and then coming back, you find it takes a while to get into things. Speaking of that . . . During our 'holiday', the touring company had come in to play in our stead. Not in our costumes, they had their own, just our stead. The Earl of Harpenden (my character) was an Ordinary Seaman. The actor who played him in the road company must have been very small. I'm no Richard Coeur de Lion in size – nor in anything much else, come to think of it, I was better casting for his brother John – but this touring Harpenden must have been a midget. Unhappily he had left his trousers behind and taken mine. I squeezed into them during a quick change, there was no moment for squeezing out – nor any others to shove on. I had to bash straight on to the stage and into a tender lover scene, wearing bell-bottoms four inches clear up from my boots.

Not only had the rhythm been broken by that holiday, the enforcement shook us actors rigid. Was this the shape of theatrical things to come? At that time, only the very grand had release clauses built into their contracts. Today – Equity insists, proudly – no actor may be compelled to stay in work for more than six months. (This in a profession where there is – fairly consistently – an unemployment figure of between eighty and ninety per cent!)

Autre temps . . . The theatre I grew up in was a place of magic where a good manager employed good actors to spirit up success. And success meant money. 'Money', today, is a theatrical mustn't. You oughtn't to think of it, you ought to be above it. Money is a thing for the State to think about. Theatres paying VAT? Put up a banner, fall in and march, it's disgraceful. (It *is*, in fact. It is ludicrous, on the face of it, to pour State money (ours) down a gaping, ever-thirsty 'artistic' drain with one hand and put out the other for something back. You, the State, should know better!)

I appeared once at a heavily subsidised theatre. A week after we had opened, I stood at the bar, happily passing the time of late night. All was cosy and the chat went from one end to the other of the long counter. We were one big artistic family, having a drink with Dad (the administrator – £7,500 per annum, rising to £10,000 – this was in the early seventies.) I happened to ask 'How's business?' You might have thought I had farted in the middle of Mass. Business? *Business?* Yes, business, how's business? (It used to be important how many tickets you sold, it had a direct bearing on how long you would go on eating.) The Administrator informed me he didn't know. Then he bought me a drink, presumably on 'expenses', and the chat began again – but haltingly, I had upset the general tenor.

All of which is not all that irrelevant. At the time *The Mousetrap* began its yearly re-casting, actors were still keen to work. There was a snag though – for them and, therefore, for the management. There would be no kudos. It was unlikely the critics would come again now that they knew whodunit. The only benefit to be derived was the likelihood – later, the certainty – of a year's work. But because the success of the enterprise was already assured by virtue of the Christie name, the financial reward could not be expected to be more than minimal. So just what was being offered?Actors and agents who though I didn't publicise my connection with the play knew of it, would badger me with questions – even accusations. All I could do was to assure them that in no sense was I operating in a managerial context. I defended to the hilt my boss's principle of nursing the play through its bad patches – and it had them – by casting some unknown actors and keeping a tight pull on the purse strings.

Something very disturbing happened finally, which shook my boat nearly to overturning. A manager wanted to engage me as director for a very different kind of play. The kind which, in fact, I needed and wanted and could have done well by. The star's reaction brought me up short when it was reported to me.

'But he,' she said to the manager, 'is the one who directs those awful Agatha Christies!'

The Christies had to that date been two in number. Both had been smash hits. I learned that success, in some fields, could be damaging.

A few more observations about long runs before I climb off my horse.

There are, I maintain, two parts to acting. Part One is being able to do it, Part Two is being able to continue doing it. 'Sustaining' it's called. To young actors of this era the word may be as dirty as 'money'. Let me assure them it's clean as a whistle. Let me, by way of some analogy, further hope that if they run into appendix trouble the surgeon – who may be removing his five hundredth – will excise it with at least as much skill as he showed in removing his first. (It might well be greater, wouldn't they think? So what's wrong with perseverance? The analogy isn't exact. The surgeon may look forward to the odd haemorrhoidectomy.)

Many a good amateur can do it very well once. (Actor, not doctor – acting is the only profession you may enter knowing nothing about it. Some even carry on carrying it off and make their final exit knowing nothing.) Twice or even three times may not be too many for the gifted amateur. In general, that's all that's needed for the Beetlebury Operatic and Dramatic. To do it for a run – even a modest run – requires an extra skill which should be part of every actor's equipment. Sadly, it isn't. On every side you hear the convenient yawning complaint: 'I can't bear long runs, can you?' Before you can't bear them, make sure you could *do* them.

It used to be fairly rare that an actor couldn't. Actors were so grateful to be in work that when they did hit a run they acquired the way of it. The 'personalities' found it more difficult. Noël Coward couldn't play a long run. Therefore he wouldn't. He would cheerfully throw everyone out of work after three months. (How happy they would be now, they weren't then!)

Six months – the present Equity maximum – may also be the limit of the modern actor's capacity. Any actor who 'gets stale' in a long run is, for me, not a fully rounded performer. It is a highly important part of his job to know how not to become stale.

The reason a modern actor gives – apart from simple boredom or the need to get back to the telly (this is valid enough, you can't make your name in the theatre any more) – is that a long run is stultifying. He needs to do something new in order to stretch himself, gain experience, make progress.

My view – and it may be old fashioned enough to be unique – is that a long run gives you superb scope for self-improvement. The discipline, the imagination, the nightly stimulus to the creative spirit demanded are just what Thespis ordered. There is nothing, absolutely nothing to equal it. Given, of course, that you are playing a good part in a good play. An actor who tells me that after three months he has given a part everything he can give is deluded. Has he taken everything, too? The national companies get their *As You Like It* practice by repetition. Unbroken repetition – a long run as distinct from seasonal tries – affords tremendous opportunities. If you know how to wash the mind clean and recreate at every performance you will experience exhilaration at new discovery. You won't want to shoot off and play another part. You'll thank the Long-Run Deity not only for your pay packet, but for the chance you keep getting to remove another appendix. Or whatever. Each time the skill becoming greater, deeper, more polished. You'll be hem-stitching.

The longest run I ever had was not more than two years . . . Maybe two and a half, *French Without Tears* might have added up to two and a half if you count Broadway. Though there was a break in between. I had something like the same in *While the Sun Shines*. I can only say that to the last performance in each case I was worrying around with the methods of whipping out those appendices and having the time of my learning life. I never, I confess, ran for anything like thirty years. *The Mousetrap – vis-à-vis* an actor's career – would be not so much a long run as a life sentence. We must except *The Mousetrap*. In reference to it, we must regard each one year stint a a long run in its own right. To sustain for a year requires skill enough.

The above applies, I think, whether the play you are playing in is, in fact, a play or a whodunit. In the latter case, you are merely engaged in a different kind of repeated exercise. A pleasant enough exercise, the Christie one. You trot your audience round the circus-ring of puzzlement, jumping them through hoops carefully prepared by author and director, making them stretch, stand on one leg, sit up and beg . . . Finally, you reward them with a pat on the head as you slip the denouement sugar lump into their mouths for being good animals. It is much the same technique as you need for keeping *Hamlet* fresh. In fact, a whodunit is a touch harder than *Hamlet*. You are nearer the surface in performance. You need two sets of reins, one to control the character, the other to control the guessing.

Speaking of guessing, I'm surprised how many people do.

Perhaps, at this stage, there is a certain amount of general knowledge. Perhaps the larger part of today's audiences goes to crow over the smaller part?

The histrionically itching feet took me off to the Hebrides to film *The Maggie*. Paul Douglas had the lead and I played a nervous, bowler-hatted and umbrellaed Englishman in his employ. The filming lasted three or four months and is one of my happier memories. A song I had written ten years earlier called *Maybe It's Because I'm a Londoner* was beginning to catch on and lawyers faded into the distance, barely to be remembered at all.

Soon after I had completed filming *The Maggie* – in 1953, Peter Saunders gave me the script of the next Christie and offered me the direction of it. It was, I think, her best. She had adapted it from a short story and I thought it looked very promising indeed. The title was *Witness for the Prosecution*.

I made a few suggestions after reading the play. Principally I felt that, in the climate of the day, it would be wrong if crime should be left paying a dividend. (Subsequently, to my astonishment, Agatha claimed that she insisted – above everything – upon retaining her original ending.) I outlined what I thought should happen and Christie incorporated the idea. Today, of course, the culprit would make an acceptable impression thumbing a nose at the acquittal verdict.

Witness for the Prosecution is the one Christie play I am sorry I didn't direct. I had other plans and they turned out not so well. I suggested Wallace Douglas to Peter. He was an old theatre friend. During wartime he wrote to me from a Prisoner-of-War camp in Germany asking me to send him some sheet music for camp entertainment. Among other pieces, I sent him the published copy of my first song, *I'm Going to Get Lit up When the Lights Go Up In London*. It wasn't until after I had posted it I remembered the words of the last chorus . . .

> I'm going to get so unsedately, so serenely stinking
> The day we finally exterminate the Huns, Huns, Huns . . .

I was convinced I had sent poor old Wally to another sort of camp. He never wrote back, so naturally I thought the worst. It transpired they were too busy tunnelling.

Wally was grateful to me and said so. His success with *Witness* led to his being invited to tackle other whodunits –and, who knows, perhaps to his long association with the comedies at the Whitehall.

The prosecuting counsel in *Witness for the Prosecution* was played by another friend, a fellow member of the Green Room Club, D.A. Clarke-Smith. Clarkie was stoking his solid fuel boiler one night when the cover shot off and hit him on the head. He was laid up but wouldn't stay long enough at home. He returned to the play too soon and died shortly afterwards. When the accident happened – and while we thought Clarkie would need only a few weeks to recover – Verity Hudson, Saunders' General Manager, mentioned the situation. I offered to take over in the meantime. She cabled Peter, who was in America setting up the deal to present *Witness* there. He cabled back one word, **YES**, and I 'prosecuted' for several weeks.

Percy Marmont played the judge. At the time of my first divorce and while his family were still in Hollywood I shared his charming house in Chelsea. I had seen him when I was at school on the screen at the Rink Cinema in Sydenham. Percy had been quite a star. He never was in *The Mousetrap* but, oddly, in the twenties he played in a movie with Clara Bow called *Mantrap*. They all had titles like that.

When I came to know him I said, 'Percy, tell me about Clara Bow . . . '

'She was marvellous,' he said. '*Mantrap*,' I said. 'What about that scene in *Mantrap* where you lifted her out of the canoe. It was unforgettable.'

'Yes,' he said. 'I won't forget it. I ruptured myself.'

Percy came into my dressing room one night. His mood was a mixture of laughter and indignation. Percy, in common with many an actor, was constantly appalled by the blinkered type-casting that went on in film studios.

'I've just been offered a part in a picture,' he said. 'It's about a court case. Know what I'm playing?'

'The judge?' I asked.

'What else?' he said. 'Freddie Hollis is in it too.' (Philip Hollis – to give him his true name – was appearing in *Witness* as the Clerk of the Court.) 'No need to guess, he's playing the Clerk of the bloody Court. And . . . ' It was here that laughter took over from indignation. ' . . . You won't believe this,' he went on after a gulpy pause

'. . . There's a character in the film . . . He's described in the script as a "bull-like man". Whom do you think they've cast?'

'Not . . . ?' I began.

'Right first time,' he said. 'Peter Bull!'

Saunders had poured quite a bit of *The Mousetrap* take into the new play. It had an impressive Old Bailey set mounted on trucks. They swung into position with a speed that frightened the life out of me backstage. If you weren't standing on your particular truck – and holding on like grim death – at the moment the swing went into operation, you got left behind. I was a newcomer to the fairground. Nobody told me the drill, I barely made it the first night. One night I didn't make it at all. The prosecuting counsel gave himself a star entrance – apparently through the court room wall. An audience doesn't notice these things. The secret is to carry it off, a touch of the old confidence is all that's needed.

Witness for the Prosecution was a thriller in the Edgar Wallace tradition, I'm convinced this was half the reason for its success. Disguise played an important part – in fact, a vital part. The other half was perhaps the inclusion of a court room scene, these seldom fail.

At the end of this refreshing and highly enjoyable stint I took off to make another movie. The letter – from Betty Box – said: 'We begin with location. We shall be cruising round the Mediterranean for two weeks on a private yacht . . . '

The film was *Doctor at Sea*. I also wrote the music for it and met Brigitte Bardot, so Christie took a back seat for a while.

Not for Saunders. She continued to be in the forefront of his productional thoughts. The following year, he presented a light whodunit called *The Spider's Web* at the Savoy Theatre. For a few weeks Agatha had three successes running in London at the same time – *Witness for the Prosecution, The Spider's Web* . . . and *The Mousetrap*.

Witness for the Prosecution closed, *The Spider's Web* closed.

The Mousetrap went on running.

At the fifth anniversary, the management threw a party on the stage at the Ambassadors' Theatre, where the play had opened. It took place immediately after a performance; the audience were asked to remain in their seats. The party was televised. Peter had invited a gathering of actors from another production of his – Cicely

Courtneidge, Naunton Wayne, Robertson Hare . . . I was asked to introduce the proceedings. There was a cake.

Five years! Unheard of. Well, not unheard of, many another play had run longer. *Chu Chin Chow* had run for four years but played to more than twice the number of people – you had to consider seating capacities. His Majesty's (*Chu Chin Chow*) – 1285, the Ambassadors' – 452. (Saunders did cram in about fifty more during the run, removing the centre aisle in the stalls.)

Abie's Irish Rose had run for nearly six years on Broadway. Lorenz Hart immortalised both the title and the achievement in a twenties song called *Manhattan* . . .

Our future babies
We'll take to *Abie's*
Irish Rose . . .
We hope they live to see it close . . .

A play called *The Drunkard* had a tremendous run in America but not without a break or a move. *Tobacco Road* opened in New York in 1933 when I was a mere student. It was still running when I played on Broadway in *French Without Tears* in 1937 and 38. It was on for nearly eight years.

Nearer home, Noël Coward's *Blithe Spirit* had run for 1997 performances – again at different theatres. Agatha's piece was blither. When she out-stripped him in the totting up stakes Noël sent a congratulatory wire that began: 'DEAR AGATHA CHRISTIE–MUCH AS IT PAINS ME . . . '

CHAPTER NINE
'The Best Thriller in Town'

A murder takes place next door to Agatha . . . No help for a newcomer and I get livid with a 'leg' . . . Death by suffocation . . . 'Wow!' and 'Wham!' – a theatre goes up in flames . . . 'The Best Thriller in Town' . . . Death of a play by suffocation.

Early in 1958 two young Canadian actors Spencer Teakle and Neil McCallum decided to present an American thriller next door at the St Martin's. They asked me whether I would agree to direct it, explaining that they were new to putting on plays and that their resources were limited. I thought it about time *The Mousetrap* had a rival so I accepted and tried to give them every possible help.

It was uphill work. Helping, I mean. Nobody – I have never understood the reason for this – welcomes newcomers in the theatre production field. I would have thought the more the healthier from every viewpoint. The more managers the greater the likelihood that theatres will remain open to provide a constant flow of plays. Nothing as damaging to the live entertainment image as a dark (closed) theatre, surely? If any one project hits the jackpot, so much the better. If the winner is a newcomer, it could be he'll stay and promote another at another theatre. This can only make for a bracing climate in the production world. It is – I would have thought – in the interest of everyone to greet with all possible encouragement a keen, bona fide theatre gambler. If he doesn't have a red carpet rolled out, at least slip him a free pass to the magic circle, let him in on a trick or two.

Teakle and McCallum had to do it the hard way. The play they had bought was a first-class – not whodunit but will-she-get-away-with-it. The authors were Audrey and William Roos. *Speaking of Murder* it was called, I hadn't heard of it but it seemed the play had had a good run in New York – perhaps at an off-Broadway theatre. I saw no reason why it shouldn't be a hit in London, it was a cracking good drama.

Teakle opened by saying he had been offered a set that had been only briefly used, could we re-vamp it for our purposes? (I remembered my jiggering about with the Ralph Lynn set for Saunders.) He showed me a photograph. The chief interest, in *Speaking of Murder* lay in a safe. This must be prominently placed because the villainess of the piece pops living things into it and slams the door. The set Teakle had been offered had a super, sweeping stairway. You began going up from Upstage Centre towards Stage Right then you turned a corner at the top and came straight towards the audience, before turning right to make an exit. The part that stood underneath this upstairs landing I adapted to take the safe so that we had this slap-on to the audience. Yes, I thought, this set would do very well. Teakle said he wanted me to be absolutely sure, I could have a new one if I insisted. (He'd gone white as he said this.) I was happy, I said, this set couldn't be bettered.

Casting. Every agent we approached added a bit to the salary of the artist we wanted – clearly they didn't believe in newcomers either. I knew to a fiver the worth of pretty well every actor or actress in Equity. Teakle and I had a code. If I scratched my nose it meant I suggested he told the agent to stuff it. My nose was quite sore by the end of the first session. One very important agent indeed – he was one leg of an octopus organisation – said he didn't represent the lady I had recommended to Teakle. Teakle reported this to me and I took over the telephone.

'Yes, you do,' I said. 'It says so here in *Spotlight*.'

Spotlight is a sort of private 'Yellow Pages' for actors only. It costs actors a bomb to have their faces in it. I don't know why agents shouldn't pay ten per cent of the bill – they get their names publicised for nothing. There is no fool like an actor.

'I'll just check,' he said and left me hanging on for three or four minutes. When at last he came back he said:

'We don't represent her.'

'I think you'll find you do,' I persevered. 'Try . . . ' and I mentioned the name of another leg of the octopus.

'Hold on a minute.'

'No,' I said. 'You ring me back . . . Or shall I have a word with . . . ' I mentioned the octopus' head.

'I'll ring you back,' he said.

In all, twenty minutes had passed before they admitted they did indeed represent the lady. I had a mental picture of the poor star, alone and untelephoned, perhaps for a year (I hadn't seen her name around for two, come to think of it). Even stars can starve. They do it with style and dissemble beautifully but they starve. After a discussion, this new 'leg' said he had never heard of Spencer Teakle or Neil McCallum. I was beginning to become lethal. My wartime death-dealing instructions do, from time to time, beg to be remembered.

'Have you heard of me?' I asked.

'Of course, dear,' he said.

'Then you must believe,' I said quietly, 'that I would not associate myself with an organisation (Teakle and McCallum) in which I do not have complete faith.'

'She'll want ten per cent of the gross,' he said.

'She has never had ten per cent of the gross in her life,' I said. (Teakle had gone white again.) 'She'll get a guarantee on account of five after we get production costs back. Call me yes or no, we have a list as long as your leg.' I meant 'arm', no wonder he seemed mystified. But my blood was up. What got me was that they wouldn't have tried it on with an established management.

Teakle – whose colour had come back – was pouring me a large Scotch from a half-bottle.

We didn't get this particular lady, she was abroad making a picture – yet another leg of the octopus had set up the deal for her.

We got ourselves a marvellous cast led by Robert Urquhart, one of my favourite actors. Maxine Audley played the villainess with suffocation on her mind and Joyce Carey gave one of her best performances as a tipsy blackmailer. The safe is an old, disused job and nobody knows the combination. Urquhart had written it down somewhere. His ten-year-old son had learnt it by heart but has made a pledge – never mind why, it's one of those kid's cross-my-heart things – not to divulge it. Maxine shoves the kid's mother (Jan Holden) in the safe. She has already suffocated the family dog, so we know it isn't a good place to spend much time – and time is ticking by. The last twenty minutes of the play have you off the edge of your seat and on to the floor and back again. In the nick, they open the safe and the wife is rescued. But there is more to come. Maxine is trying to escape but her way is blocked. For a moment she moves into the open doorway of the safe. She is about to come out when her path is blocked by Urquhart, in a furious temper with himself. Unseen, she dodges back into the safe. Urquhart curses the damn thing and says he's going to have it bricked up tomorrow. As he says this he slams the door – on Maxine – and gives a savage turn to the lock. I had a pin spot on this spinning lock. The stage is filled with characters, all talking and shouting at once but all we are conscious of is that the woman inside the safe will be there forever. The lock goes on spinning as the curtain falls.

I have never known a first night to equal it. Nor a more enthusiastic press. The headline in the *Daily Express* read: WOW! THE ENDING TOOK MY BREATH AWAY. John Barber was the critic. He went on to say:

> I have never known a thriller end like this. It builds up to a thunderclap surprise that took my breath away. Then down swung the curtain and up went the applause . . . It was as surprising as seeing the stage burst into flames.

The headline in the *Evening News* said: THIS LEAVES US GASPING. The *Standard* notice was headlined THE PLOT AND PACE MAKE THIS FIRST RATE and went on:

> Through the sheer ingenuity of its plot and the brisk pace at which these menacing items are skilfully juggled, *Speaking of Murder* ranks as a first rate thriller.

The *Kensington News* called it 'The best thriller in town' and the *Queen* went further to say, 'This is one of the best thrillers I have seen on the stage'.

Here we had an interesting situation. The juxtaposition of *The Mousetrap* and 'the best thriller in town' . . . One by Agatha Christie, the other by two unknowns. The Ambassadors' Theatre had some pretty good notices – painted upon boards. The St Martin's Theatre put them in the shade with one-word quotes like 'WOW' and 'WHAM'. Would the newcomer measure up in commercial attraction?

I had designed the *Speaking of Murder* bill myself. We used a photograph of Maxine – a large head, no neck, just the head – but printed negative. This, blown up to a huge size, arrested you very effectively as you approached the front of the theatre. Further, we had the good luck to land a television preview the night before the opening. About eight minutes. I wrote a capsule version, not, of course, giving the final game away, and introduced it myself. The show was *Chelsea at Nine*, televised from the old Chelsea Palace, a peak spot at that time. This – together with the rave press – gave us packed houses.

The month was June. The weather was warm. These were days before tourism changed the face of the London box-office scene. It was still the fashion to play it very cagey in summer time. The entrenched successes were relatively safe, a new show was out on a sunny limb. Still . . . our box-office was as busy as the one next door – perhaps busier. For a while. Then the heat began to tell.

At these times you appreciate the importance of careful – even niggardly – budgeting. A shrewd commercial manager may scrape by, not making, not losing. Until the weather cools and a breeze blows into the ticket department. The box office likes equability. A blast of heat, a touch of blizzard . . . even too hard a downpour . . . these are to be dreaded. A manager watches the weather as a night driver watches the white line in the middle of the road. If you get rain, you mustn't get it too late or the customers won't leave home. A shower early in the day will put them off thinking about walks, picnics – any nonsense like that. They book for a show. But a shower too late if they haven't booked . . . If it happens about six o'clock and isn't too heavy, well and good . . . Then there are things like Motor Shows – good, they'll come in the evening. Wakes Weeks – bad, there's nobody in town (this is when you're on the road). Strikes? Disaster if they're on the railway or the tube. If they're on the telly – hurrah!

It was just the heat that hit the *Speaking of Murder* box-office. Despite the help I was able to give him, Teakle had over-budgeted to the extend of about a hundred pounds a week. The receipts dropped – but only to a point where he was losing just that amount . . . If only we could have ticked over. A hundred a week – it sounds like nothing today but money was then worth money – to a young, new management was a significant amount to be losing. After about six of these – with the summer showing no signs of being unkind to holiday makers, namely kind to us . . . we – 'the best thriller in town' – were forced to a closure. It did occur to me to wonder what effect, if any, would be created by a disappearance of Audrey and William Roos. I reflected that what made headlines in the twenties probably wouldn't, in the late fifties, even make the STOP PRESS!

The Mousetrap went on running.

CHAPTER TEN

The Unexpected Guest

Diary of a Who-body ... I consider the New Wave on a Portuguese beach ... 'The Unexpected Guest' ... I lay an egg in the sun and won't wait for Godot ... A lesson in whodunitry ... I put on the dog and fall flat on my dry ice ... 'Who Killed Agatha Christie?' ... Agatha jumps from a box to the Dress Circle and we have another palpable hit.

Speaking of Murder – by Audrey and William Roos – opened at the St Martin's Theatre in June of 1958 and ran for about three months. My next Christie venture opened in August of the same year and would break all previous box-office records at the Duchess Theatre with a run of more than six hundred performances.

We were now thirty-two years away from the disappearance ... and thirty years away from Agatha's entry into the theatre. Her novels were appearing at yearly intervals. Her theatre diary looked like this:

1928 *Alibi* adapted by Michael Morton from *The Murder of Roger Ackroyd*. 250 performances at the Prince of Wales' Theatre. (Laughton as Poirot.)

1930 *Black Coffee* written by Agatha as a play. (Nothing whatever to do with Roger Ackroyd.)

1936 *Love from a Stranger*: adapted from Agatha's short story *Philomel Cottage* by Frank Vosper who also starred in it at the New. I saw the production and was struck by the theatricality (Edgar Wallace, again!).

1940 *Peril at End House*: dramatized by Arnold Ridley the actor who wrote *The Ghost Train* (and later adorned *Dad's Army*).

1943 *Ten Little Niggers*: Dramatized by Agatha herself. This was a good one, I thought. I saw it at a matinée when I was on leave. The theatre was half empty. I was pleased enough – on my soldier's pay – to get a free seat but – the poorness of the business surprised me. Other theatres were packing them in. Musicals, though – mostly. And the play I was to join later, *While the Sun Shines*. Maybe the war was thriller enough?

1945 *Appointment with Death*: Agatha's adaptation.

1946 *Murder on the Nile*: as above. At the Ambassadors'. I tried to get a part in it but there was nothing doing. There wasn't much doing at the theatre after it opened.

1950 *Murder at the Vicarage*: dramatized by M. Charles and B. Toy. At the Playhouse. Miss Marple. (Agatha had created her in the hope she would see old Poirot out. Poirot seemed to have her readership in thrall, he wasn't easy to see out.) This was the last Christie before Saunders took over and made her what, today, is called a 'superstar'. It occurs to me that Saunders did for Agatha in the theatre what the disppearance had achieved for her at the bookshop. The disappearance, however, continuing to help.

1951 *The Hollow*: 376 performances at the Fortune and Ambassadors' Theatres. Followed by . . .

1952 *The Mousetrap*: Agatha's wireless play, extended by her. It began at the Ambassadors', then moved next door to the St Martin's.

1953 *Witness for the Prosecution*: adapted by Agatha from her own short story. Perhaps her best. 478 performances at the Winter Garden Theatre (it used to be in Drury Lane). When it crossed the Atlantic it won an award from the New York critics.

1954 (Since *The Hollow* we're coming into one a year, as with the books!)

The Spider's Web: written by Agatha as a play for Margaret Lockwood. Savoy Theatre, 774 performances. Miss Lockwood had never disappeared but had made a solid impact that served her well on the stage.

1956 (What happened to '55?)

Towards Zero: dramatized by Agatha and Gerald Verner. The St James's again – not a big success. It is customary to blame the out-of-the-wayness of theatres like the St James's for a failure. *The Frog* – by Edgar Wallace – was a smash hit at one of London's most blamed houses, the Prince's (now called the Shaftesbury).

It was on a beach in the Algarve, Portugal, that I began casting *The Unexpected Guest.*

I had gone to Portugal to buy land on which I would later build a house. In common with others of my age – and experience – I had come to look upon theatrical developments and the swamping of old Thespis by New Waves with a wary eye. This might, many of us had begun to think, be get-out-while-the-getting's-good time. It was a moment – and one that threatened to become an aeon – when entertainment was out and the dustbin was in. The revolution – begun by Osborne's boring little man looking back in a pet – had razed things nicely to the ground. All were now agog to see what would rise in their place.

Coward had been clipped by Pinter, Beckett had rubbed out Rattigan. White ties and tails surrendered to no ties and sweat-shirts. Technique gave place to the grunt, the graceful gesture to the scratch. A witty line lost out to an interminable pause. What, we wondered, were we waiting for? Not that old Godot? One thing was certain amid the shifting sands – nobody, but nobody was going to spring *The Mousetrap.*

I sat on this beach . . .

If I could have been content with living on royalties (strangely, the yearning by expatriates the world over for London would have enabled me to live as an expatriate) and writing the days away, this escape might have worked well. I was fond enough of scribbling. But I had this urge for personal involvement. It would be too awful to write, say, a play and send it off to England or America and leave the rest to others.

If it were bought it might be by the wrong management – one with no taste, by Salazar! There are these. He might cast it wrongly, set it wrongly. Have it wrongly directed by a director who would fiddle. (I might fiddle, of course, with Christie but God help anyone who fiddled – unbidden – with me. Here's an odd thing, now. In London one might be tempted to be grateful for a sale. Away in the sun you are God – not Godot, you're there, there's no waiting – to yourself and all your works are masterpieces.) I decided the situation – were I to indulge it – would have problems as a cave has stalactites. And stalag*mites* – sticking up where they shouldn't.

In '58, though, I still had these dreams. One had to think of something, make the odd panic preparation. (Who could know that this New Wave, having made the shore mucky, would retreat as though Neptune had pulled the stopper?)

I sat on this beach . . .

Saunders had telephoned me to say he was sending his General Manager out with a script. Would I read it at once. She was also bringing the two fat volumes of *Spotlight*. If I liked the play would I make casting suggestions.

So much expenditure – Verity Hudson was there for almost more than a day, I recall – bespoke strong managerial faith in the project and every hope that we could bring it off yet again. Charity didn't come into it.

Agatha had written *The Unexpected Guest* as a play. Her adaptation of *The Hollow* had awarded me, first, a heart tremor then weeks of day and night slavery. Before we even got into rehearsal. *The Unexpected Guest* had its problems. But they were new problems – the old 'I'll-put-the-kettle-on' – exit – enter – 'The-kettle's-boiling' bit was nowhere in evidence. Much thought had been given to this Guest . . . much attention having been paid to the manipulation of that Hollow.

Briefly, the story . . . (If you have ever tried to tell the story of a Christie work, you will appreciate the meaning of the aposiopesis.) We are in South Wales, near the Bristol Channel. Thick fog outside. It clears as the play progresses but the fog within thickens and the tale has more twists than the Welsh lanes Michael Starkwedder gets lost in. That's his name. He is the 'Unexpected Guest'. The lights of his car flash across the window (French again) . . . after a moment he looms up outside, knocks – finds the window open and comes in. The room is in darkness. Hiding against a wall, gun in hand, is the attractive Mrs Warwick.

Warwick is present too, sitting in an invalid chair. Starkwedder explains to him that he ran his car into a ditch in the fog and is lost. He has quite a chat with Warwick before it dawns on him the fellow's dead. 'Here's a pretty kettle of fish,' he thinks – we think. He sees the wife. He's going to make sure this time so he waits for a couple of answers. He sees the gun, she doesn't hide it. She confesses to murder. Warwick was a drunken sadist, she couldn't bear it any longer. 'Sit down,' says Starkwedder, 'have a drink.'

'What about calling the police?' she puts in.

'Not yet,' he says, looking her up and down, 'tell me all about it.' So she does do.

Starkwedder (this will be easier when we get on to first name terms) – as we see it and hear it – falls both for her and her story and decides to help her.

A man named MacGregor – red haired, red bearded, from Canada . . . threatened Warwick two years ago, we learn. Warwick – drunk at the wheel – had run over MacGregor's kiddywink but had been acquitted. Starkwedder pins a note on the dead man's chest (thorax) . . . He makes it up with letters cut from a newspaper and pasted onto a writing sheet. The note will point to MacGregor. (It occurs to us that, if the police catch up with this Celt, he's going to have a devil of a job explaining since he won't know what they're on about.)

Warwick – big game hunter, lionised and now in a wheel-chair – is a nut who sits at this window nightly, shooting at this and that. In default of cats, rabbits and the odd charity worker he shoots his initials into the dado. Starkwedder sends Laura (Mrs W.) upstairs to get into a nightie.

'Give me four minutes,' he says (why not five?), 'then you'll hear a shot . . . I'll shove a full stop after those initials. Then I'll blow. You react as you would if none of this had already happened. Come down with the startled household. Leave the rest to me.'

Off goes Laura to stick the cut newspaper in the Aga, change and wake up the housekeeper for an aspirin. (Not only is she going to be in need of this, it will provide an alibi. The two will be together when they hear the shot.)

Starkwedder uses the four minutes to clean the room of fingerprints and make things look as normal as possible, given there's a lionised stiff Right Centre. He checks his watch, fires his full stop and exit into the Welsh fog.

Down comes the household. They find the body, Starkwedder knocks on the window, comes in and says, 'What's going on?' 'Wait a minute,' they say, 'who are you?' and he tells them the same tale he tried to get through to the dead man, and then told Laura. His car is in a ditch, he's lost, he came up to the house for help. On his way, he adds this time, he heard a shot. 'Then out comes this running figure, collides with me and drops this . . . (the gun).'

Everybody – except the policeman, Christie wouldn't do that to us twice, we reason – is under suspicion. The police think it's MacGregor, we know it isn't. Then . . . they learn that MacGregor died in Alaska soon after his return there from England. (Just as well, we feel, he'd have been on a sticky wicket.) It wasn't MacGregor but it must be someone who knew about him and his threats. They swoop back upon the household.

At last, Jan, the young, half-witted half-brother whom Warwick had threatened to commit to an asylum, confesses. (We see through this, it is bravado prompted by suggestion. We put money, in fact, on the old housekeeper who does the suggesting.) Jan runs off, waving one of the dead man's guns and is shot accidentally in a struggle to recapture him.

'The best way out,' says the Inspector. 'Goodnight, all.'

Laura and Starkwedder are left alone. He's 'Michael' by now. Laura is distressed about the boy. 'It wasn't Jan,' says Michael, 'that was suggestion, it could have been anybody. Even MacGregor.'

'MacGregor's dead,' says Laura.

'Well, of course,' says Michael, 'but I can make out a case for his having done it . . . '

Then Starkwedder . . . Michael . . . tells the story as it might have happened:

> MacGregor, planning revenge, shaves off his beard, dies his hair . . . drops his accent? 'Arranges' his death in Alaska and pops over to Bristol. Or South Wales. He drives up to the house and confronts Warwick. Both have guns, W. fires and misses (but he is a crack shot!) MacGregor doesn't miss. Having dealt ballistic retribution and avenged his kiddywink, exit quickly to his car for a getaway . . . But he drives into a ditch. (Understandably, he's overwrought.) What to do now . . . but come back to the house as a lost stranger . . . 'discover' the body . . .

'You speak as though you know just what happened,' says Laura.

'Of course I know,' says Michael S. 'Don't you understand? I'm MacGregor!'

Crash. Michael kisses Laura. She hasn't really had time to take it in but she isn't going to get time, we've had the denouement and he's off.

I said there were problems. The first is what do you tell your leading actor, your Michael Starkwedder? Now that we know the ending, the beginning doesn't make any kind of sense. This MacGregor . . . has done the deed, hopped in his car and driven straight into a ditch. He decides to come back and arrives at the house a second time, not mentioning his recent encounters with the owner.

Does he come to the front door, ring the doorbell, wake the house to ask for help? Not on your life. Nor Warwick's. He sidles in through this French window . . . into a pitch dark room. It was empty when he left it except for the late big game hunter. He doesn't know that Laura has entered, checked on her old man's state of health, picked up the gun . . . heard him coming and hidden.

So, what does he do? Shout up the stairs that he has come to the house for help and found a dead man (not a bad second for normality if he must come through that window)? No, no. He stops to pass the time of night with the corpse! Now, who chats with a corpse? A nut? A nut-to-nut chat? But this Starkwedder is such a sane, clear-thinking lad, he's no nut. He's a mere kiddywink-avenger. Sympathy we are expected to have.

In the case of *The Mousetrap*, we have a raving looney who plays a part through to the denouement. Starkwedder isn't acting. For his own benefit, I mean. For ours, yes, he's acting his Canadian socks off to hoodwink us. But . . . how do we play this opening? He is acting for any possible listening ears? Thin . . . but all we can offer.

I sat on this beach . . . We both did, Verity Hudson and I.

I needed a first class actor for Starkwedder, clearly. (One needs first class actors for every part and tries – within the budget – to get them. Sometimes the purse-strings nip your fingers as you dip.) 'Nigel Stock?' I said. Verity agreed, at once. Would he want too much in the way of salary, though? 'Whatever he asks,' I said . . . 'he's worth double.'

I stretched out in the Algarve sun, feeling like a hen who has succeeded in laying a large, important egg.

Back went Miss Hudson to London. I followed as soon as I could, this was to be my first Christie-from-scratch since *The Hollow*. I wanted to do at least as much for it.

I learned that Nigel Stock liked the play – and, of course, the part. You could make a meal of Starkwedder and never more go hungry. Of its kind, it *is* a good part. It isn't of the classics, it isn't Hamlet, nor Marchbanks. It isn't a classic whodunit, not in the same league as *Witness for the Prosecution*. Nor *The Ringer*. But it's good.

We marked out a super cast, I didn't think we'd stand an earthly of getting them all. We got most.

Renée Asherson – an old friend of mine from days when we were both at the Webber-Douglas School of Singing and Dramatic Art (its original title!) – played Laura. And made us see, at once, the reason for Starkwedder getting out the scissors and paste.

Violet Farebrother was Mama, Winifred Oughton the housekeeper. Each a peach. Paul Curran played Angell, the male nurse. Later he would be a National Theatre player. He would bring up the standard there noticeably.

Roy Purcell played the neighbour who is in love with Laura until he discovers – or thinks he discovers – that she is the guilty one. He made the brightest of red herrings. Christopher Sandford – excellent as the retarded lad.

Michael Golden and Tenniel Evans did well by the constabulary. (I made Tenniel Evans a bardic Sergeant, having him quote Keats. I even wrote some lines of bad verse for him to have composed and jotted in his note book.)

A word of staggered admiration, too, for Philip Newman who played Warwick. When I say 'played' I speak of a performance. It's easy to *overplay* a corpse. By, for instance, sneezing. He underplayed beautifully. Mind you, I did help there. Christie had him facing the audience, she described his appearance in detail. No, I said – firmly. For two reasons. Firstly, half an hour is a long time for an actor to hold his breath. (All right, put him under a rug so you don't see the in-out, up-down – he might get cramp. What does a corpse do about cramp?) Secondly . . . every eye in the theatre is going to be watching for a movement, waiting for him to go blue and what not, humans are that way inclined. Especially the kind of humans who find murder engrossing. I put him facing upstage – an actor looking down at the dead man would be facing us, he it was who would tell us about the appearance. When Nigel peered at Warwick we could see through his eyes the horror before him.

Nigel Stock – like Robert Urquhart – is a special actor. (Remarkably, I have not seen either at the National Theatre. They must have appeared there – perhaps when I was out of the country.) We had enormous fun with the first act. In particular with the long solo scene in which he removes traces of his presence in the room. I suggested a piece of business which he managed superbly – he even got it mentioned in a notice. He goes about the room cleaning off finger-prints with a handkerchief. He reconstructs his every earlier movement, working with meticulous care, cleaning, over-looking a light switch or a door-plate, going back to it . . . (The decanter and glass he doesn't clean. They bear both his and Laura's prints but to clean them free of any would draw police attention. He solves the matter soon after his phoney re-entrance.

'You look pale,' he says to Laura, 'drink this.' And he pours for her, leaving justifiable prints on decanter and glass.)

He cleans the desk with especial care. Here it was that he cut sections from the newspaper and pasted them on to a small letter-sheet. The scissors, the paste bottle . . . the writing pad . . . While he is concentrating he stumbles against the desk chair. He steadies it with his hand. Nobody in your whodunit audience will fail to notice this. So we string them along. He continues with his cleaning – everywhere in the room, everything he has touched . . . with the exception of that chair. He is ready to fire the shot and make his exit. A last look round . . . his eye lights on the chair. He pauses. Then he goes to the chair and cleans off those accidental prints. It was a very satisfying moment both for Nigel and me. (As a bonus I had him fire the shot, make a hurried move to the window . . . pause . . . realise the light should be turned off . . . raise his ungloved hand to the switch, pause before he touches it . . . then use his handkerchief to flick the switch. Exit.

I did tackle Agatha about the name chosen by this MacGregor fellow. I mean . . . 'Starkwedder'! Her answer was a superb lesson in whodunitry. It showed, as nothing could more clearly, the way the master mind works when it practises to deceive. She answered me:

'Nobody would invent a name like "Starkwedder". Anyone calling himself "Starkwedder" must be genuine.'

You don't, of course, examine it too deeply. This is the author in relation to her audience. What about MacGregor in relation to his?

What makes *him* think of a name like Starkwedder. He had a great-aunt who married a Boer, I told Nigel.

Lighting was a major problem. It needn't have been, I made it so. Since *The Hollow* I had played in some half a dozen movies and I was Johnny Head-in-air. I was getting bored with these bits of canvas propped up by sticks and the twelve spots on that bloody bar. Why couldn't we have what they gave us in the film studios? Solid-looking stonework! It was the Disney *Robin Hood* that began it. The sky was the limit in his budgeting – and a very beautiful sky it was. (I think I was ripe for subsidy.)

Peter Finch played the Sheriff of Nottingham, newly created so by me, John Plantagenet. (My brother, Coeur de Lion, having nipped off to the Crusades, if you recall?) Nottingham Castle was my pad. We opened on a battlement. That stonework! If I'd been a bit of moss, I'd have grown on it and in it. Behind us was a beautifully painted cloth, delicately lit . . . And the invention! As we looked down we saw – still painted on this cloth – a road winding away into the distance. Ken Annakin, the director, explained that there were small holes punched in the road, irregularly. Dim lights, moving slowly from low down to high up on the cloth – behind it . . . would give the illusion of a torchlight procession fading slowly up and over the hill.

Another thing they do well in movies is fog. Dry ice they use. Most effective – whether it smokes about Gene Kelly's dancing feet or is used, actually, to simulate fog.

At the opening of *The Unexpected Guest* Agatha mentions fog 'swirling' outside the window. 'Another Christie-ism,' I should have said to myself, 'she thinks she's writing a book. Forget it.' I wouldn't have listened. 'Dry ice,' I said to Saunders.

'Really?' he asked, impressed.

'Really,' I said, laying it on thick. 'We use it all the time in pictures.'

Not on the stage though, it doesn't work on the stage. Not in a play, in a room. Why? Because it billows in through the glassless windows, that's why. Even if you put glass in the windows – or something to serve as glass – it would still make its entrance through a crack wherever it found one. And you can find plenty with all those bits of canvas propped up by sticks. It might swirl on from the open wings.

(Right) Casting *The Unexpected Guest* in Portugal. Having suggested Nigel Stock for the leading part 'I stretched out in the Algarve sun, feeling like a hen who has succeeded in laying a large, important egg'.

(Below) The card Agatha posted to me from somebody's tomb. I was about to open in *Chrysanthemum*—and was at the same time deeply enmeshed in *The Unexpected Guest*.

DUCHESS THEATRE

Catherine Street, Aldwych, W.C.2 — **Telephone: TEMple Bar 8243-4**

Managing Agents: Theatre Managers Ltd. — Licensed by the Lord Chamberlain to E. W. Crossley Taylor

For times and prices please see overleaf

By arrangement with Theatre Managers Ltd.

Peter Saunders presents

RENEE ASHERSON
NIGEL STOCK
VIOLET FAREBROTHER

IN

The Unexpected Guest

by Agatha Christie

with

WINIFRED OUGHTON
CHRISTOPHER SANDFORD
MICHAEL GOLDEN
PAUL CURRAN
TENNIEL EVANS - PHILIP NEWMAN
and
ROY PURCELL

Directed by HUBERT GREGG

Décor by MICHAEL WEIGHT

Billing for *The Unexpected Guest*. John Barber wrote: ‘Only seven weeks after Agatha Christie’s last play (*Verdict*) was booed off the stage the old lady of 66 stumped defiantly back into a London Theatre last night. She heard the kind of applause that had given her *Mousetrap* a record six year run’.

No dry ice. I stuck to Number 60 Grey in the floods.

The clown wants to play Hamlet. (Today, quite often, he does.) The thriller writer wishes he or she doesn't have to thrill. Laudably, Agatha had her go in a play called *Verdict*. It didn't work. The public will take an unexpected guest but not an unexpected Christie. Its failure must have been a disappointment to Saunders who presented it. I don't think it can have been a surprise.

The operation, however, was not a good augury for us. Let's say it gave us one more hurdle than we needed. We were to clear it with feet to spare.

We opened *The Unexpected Guest* at the Bristol Hippodrome. Agatha's telegam to me remembered our thunder and lightning 'clash', in *The Hollow* – surprisingly with humour:

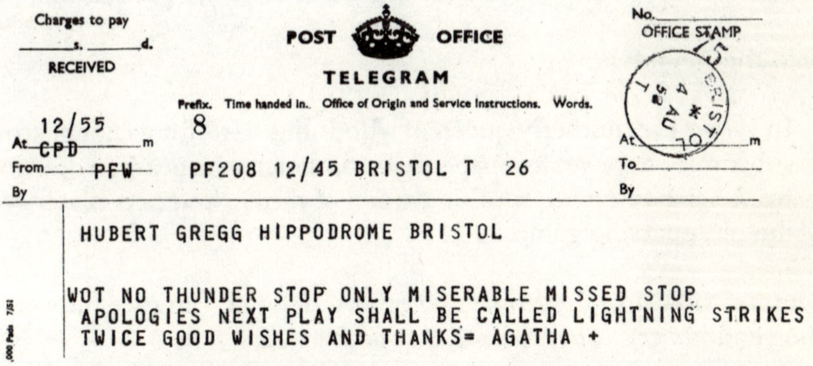

Charges to pay
s. d.
RECEIVED

POST OFFICE
TELEGRAM

No.
OFFICE STAMP

Prefix. Time handed in. Office of Origin and Service Instructions. Words.

12/55 8
At CPD m
From PFW PF208 12/45 BRISTOL T 26
By

At m
To
By

HUBERT GREGG HIPPODROME BRISTOL

WOT NO THUNDER STOP ONLY MISERABLE MISSED STOP
APOLOGIES NEXT PLAY SHALL BE CALLED LIGHTNING STRIKES
TWICE GOOD WISHES AND THANKS= AGATHA +

The Bristol Hippodrome was a vast musical house. My designer Michael Weight asked me whether he should open the set out, do his best to fill the huge stage. This would have meant re-spacing the furniture, too. We could have ended up looking like *No, No, Nanette*. I said, 'No, no, Michael. Mask in at the sides, let the actors play to the exact measurements they'll be confined to one week from now in London.' The theatre we were bound for in the metropolis was the wee Duchess. Our set had been designed specifically for its restricted stage. When we set up on the Bristol Hippodrome stage the play looked like a peep show. I didn't care. It would have been ludicrous for the cast to spend a week adjusting their moves to suit an opened out setting, then readjust for London. I wanted them to arrive at the Duchess 'played in' and relaxed. They did and were.

The critics were delighted with us. In particular, they were delighted that Agatha Christie had abandoned her recent new style in favour of the hemlock-as-before. (In this case, the revolver.) *The Financial Times* began its notice: 'Miss Agatha Christie, to everyone's relief, returns to her old ways and her old form. The curtain rises on a body . . . '

'SO MISS CHRISTIE PLAYS SAFE' was the headline in the *Herald*. *The Daily Telegraph* said:

> After the failure of her last play, *Verdict*, it was suggested in some quarters that Scotland Yard ought to be called in to discover who killed Agatha Christie. But *The Unexpected Guest*, turning up last night at the Duchess before even the reverberations of her last failure have died away, indicates that the corpse is still very much alive. Burial of her thriller reputation is certainly premature.

Said the *Daily Mail*:

> In *Verdict* the motherly queen of whodunits tried for a change to substitute character for suspense but last night she beamed down from her box on the routine parade of thriller puppets playing the old guessing game.

The *Star* (now, like the *Herald* and others, defunct – how we missed the vendor's cry: '*Star, News* a' *Standard!*') said:

> After her recent failure – with *Verdict* – to climb into a higher dramatic bracket, Agatha Christie has reverted to the old 'whodunit' formula that has paid her so well in *The Mousetrap* . . . After six wrong guesses on who did it most people will feel like crossing their fingers and crying 'Pax'. But that will not stop them from gasping at the final adroit twist that sent me home grumbling 'Fooled again' and wondering how long it will be before Miss Christie gets round to making the corpse do the murder in one of her plays . . . '

(She had used this ploy long since in *Ten Little Niggers*. I beg their pardons, 'Indians'.) John Barber, writing in the *Manchester Guardian* said:

Only seven weeks after Agatha Christie's last play was booed off the stage the old lady of 66 stumped defiantly back into a London theatre last night.

She had a new whodunit ready. She watched from the back of the circle, white-faced and apprehensive . . . [She must have nipped round there from the box]. But no boos came this time. No rude interruptions. At the end she heard the kind of applause that has given her *Mousetrap* a record six-year run.

CHAPTER ELEVEN

Go Back for Murder

Poison by oysters . . . I lay an egg in a Mousetrap . . . Death by Television – a hit musical bites the dust . . . Agatha goes back for murder and I smell a similarity . . . She 'loses her corkscrew' but gains a million . . . We take seven curtain calls and suffer death by envy.

Later in the same year I was starred in my first musical, *Chrysanthemum*, at the Prince of Wales' so I had my hands pretty full. To say nothing of my feet. Alfred Rodrigues arranged some terrific – and terrifically strenuous – choreography. But I continued to keep a witching brief over *The Mousetrap*. At the sixth anniversary we were given cloth-bound copies of the play. (It had been published. All the world might read it and become privy to the identity of the killer. It was an 'acting edition'. But woe betide any amateur or repertory company who thought of putting the issue to such a use. Nobody might perform *The Mousetrap* until close of play in London. The film rights were sold to Victor Savile but they didn't do him any good. It might not be filmed either. Poor Victor was outrun by the play and never got his money back.) Agatha presented the volume to me. Or rather, Saunders presented one to her and she passed it on – signing it with a few kind words on the fly-leaf.

Six years . . . And we seemed set for seven . . .

Each November there was a ritual luncheon . . . there probably still is . . . attended by both the outgoing and incoming tide of actors. (Directors, too, now? I managed to stay at the wicket for seven years before I carried my bat but I believe they come in and out annually these days. A matter of stamina? I'm amazed, looking back, at mine. But then we are a pretty remarkable generation.) Sometimes Christie attended. She rarely attended the first night by the new company – the gesture would have been appreciated. One year she did and I heard the following exchange of dialogue at the fall of the final curtain . . .

'Mrs Christie!'

'Yes?'

'I'm so proud of myself. I guessed right away!'

Christie (bridling more than a little): 'Oh, really? You must be familiar with my work.'

Lady (*brightly*), 'No! I've never read any of it!'

One year some of the cast ate oysters at the luncheon. They were poisoned and unable to play that evening. One of them was heard to observe later:

'We didn't mind so much being poisoned. But we got docked a night's pay!'

The story may be apocryphal.

I had been on at the management to provide a new stage carpet. It was getting threadbare. Like the American's shoes in *While the Sun Shines* and old Cristow's flannels in *The Hollow*, this carpet had given of its best. Pretty soon, for the actors, the phrase 'on the boards' would take on a new meaning, I feared. Then it happened. Without my foreknowledge, like a birthday surprise. (Only it wasn't. Just another rehearsal Monday at Monkswell Manor.) This brand new carpet. I won't say it was a deep-pile carpet, it wasn't, but it was a sight deeper than the one that had been put out to grass. Or stud (to produce little rugs, somewhere?). We rehearsed on it. With some care, nobody wanted to walk about. I rallied the cast.

'Come along,' I said. 'It'll stand up to it, I think. It's what it was made for. Now, who's going to be the first to cross Downstage Left?'

Then we broke for coffee. One of the actors was checking in his holdall. He'd come up from the country . . . (God knows why – he should have stayed there and farmed or whatever. He was a good actor but I felt for him. He used to arrive in the morning looking so healthy and go home looking like a man who'd been dead for three days.) He had these beautiful new laid eggs.

'Did you know" I asked the company, 'that if you hold an egg, end-on, between the palms of your hands . . . ' I took one and demonstrated as I spoke . . . ' . . . No matter how hard you press, you can't break it?'

I had done this trick a hundred times, it isn't a trick, it's a piece of science. And it had never failed. Until this morning. It must have had an uncommonly thin shell, this egg, that's all I can say – it shattered and shed its contents over the carpet. Centre stage. It's one of several things Saunders has never forgiven me for.

Success covers a multitude of eggs cracked. Even end to end, when they should by the book of rules remain as infrangible as a very mousetrap. I had pulled it off a second time at the Duchess (from scratch, a second time), we were a smash hit and I was the white-headed boy. (I was, in fact, beginning to go white at speed.)

Accordingly, I was invited to direct yet another Christie to follow *The Unexpected Guest*.

I didn't mind one little bit. *Chrysanthemum*, the musical in which I had co-starred with Pat Kirkwood (the superb artist to whom I was then married) had opened like a Chelsea Flower Show bloom only to close within six months. The show suffered from managerial juggling. We played for three months in a too large, unsuitable theatre then moved to a too small unsuitable one. Further, we were exposed to the television millions, a fatality which Pat and I were powerless to side-step.

Chrysanthemum was presented by Sandor Gorlinsky, a brilliant concert impresario. Sandor was a charming, gentle character. A man of integrity who I didn't think should be buffeted by the commercial theatre. It was his first experience with a stage musical. At the Prince of Wales', our landlord was Bernard Delfont, an old friend of Pat and myself. Bernie also ran a weekly television programme called *Sunday Night at the Prince of Wales'*. He wanted Pat and me to appear on it in an excerpt from the show.

Saunders advised me against accepting. 'A TV excerpt makes a straight play,' he said, 'but ruins a musical. Look at *Fanny*!' I didn't need to, I remembered. Mind you, I don't recall that *Fanny* had anything like the press *Chrysanthemum* had been greeted with. We came into the Prince of Wales' on the heels of a flop, unannounced. Our only hope was a rave press to put us over to the public. We got it. But I agreed with Peter on the general principle. Musicals – and I think this is the reason one should keep them off TV as a sheer advertising exercise – lose so much by reduction to the small screen. Why does the public go to a stage musical? For breadth of canvas, for movement. Colour. (We were still in black and white.) A straight play benefits, conversely, because you want to get closer to the characters, to see detail. It's the difference between displaying a mural as distinct from a fine pencil drawing.

If Saunders had been in partnership with Gorlinsky he might have been able to persuade Bernie of the unwisdom of putting our little pastiche on TV. But the newcomer – as with Teakle and MacCallum who presented *Speaking of Murder* – was on his own. Pat and I had no choice. We agreed in order to oblige Gorlinsky, who asked us in order to oblige Bernie.

Chrysanthemum was a romp of a melodrama set in the ragtime era. Apart from any other consideration, it would be murderously difficult to convey the charm and delicacy of the original on this comparatively new, small medium. TV was devastatingly omnipresent in the British home but, at that time, was dedicated to cheap entertainment and panel games.

The final blow was that we were to be allotted twelve minutes only. We didn't stand a hope of putting over the kind of show we were in this short time. Gorlinsky asked me to write a few Pearl White-ish captions to suggest the flavour of the piece. I did this but I don't think it helped. We followed Jimmy Wheeler, which didn't help either. We had been playing to excellent business. The week following the TV excerpt we dropped £1,700 at the box office. We had built up a big advance following the notices and now we had to draw heavily on this. Door trade had dropped alarmingly.

We moved to the Apollo Theatre where I had been ten years earlier in a marathon runner called *Off the Record*. One of the stage hands greeted me after the first night with: 'What a marvellous show, Mr Gregg. We didn't expect it to be after watching it on TV.' As I see it, we had gone on television and as good as told ten million people not to come. (By way of rough comparison, *The Mousetrap* – playing to capacity at the Ambassadors' – would take something like fifty years to gain the same exposure.)

So I was ready for one more Christie smash hit – it seemed she and I together were becoming a theatrical sure bet? I was to learn – yet again – that, in the theatre, the only sure thing is, as Irving Berlin put it succinctly in a song, 'the closing when the customers don't come'.

The Unexpected Guest had proved to be solid and workable. It had been written, by Agatha, for the stage. I hoped she had now come up with another. Her card to me wishing me luck in *Chrysanthemum* had been despatched from some archaeological digging.

Was this new one going to be *Murder in the Tomb?* No. That wasn't the title. I picked up the script to read: *Go Back for Murder* . . . All right enough, I thought. What new idea has she produced inspired by all that Middle-eastery? None . . . She had taken a story she had published in 1942, called *Five Little Pigs* and rehashed it as a play. She had indeed 'gone back for murder'.

It wasn't bad. It was different, very different but it wasn't bad. I supposed it might have been better as a novel. I had no intention of reading the book. Not until the play had opened, certainly. I hadn't with *The Hollow*. With Christie I wore theatrical blinkers, it was the only way. I knew – don't ask me how but I did – that, as with *The Hollow*, Poirot had featured in the novel but had been cut out of the play. Poor old Hercule was being eased out, he had to face it. Once more, I was happy not to have his *parlez-vous*-ing about the place. But as I read and read . . . and considered . . . something else was emerging like an object black and curly out of Loch Ness. It had the same quality of now-you-see-it, now-you-don't.

Go Back for Murder was about a wife who had killed her husband sixteen years earlier for having an affair with another woman. Or had she? The husband was irresponsible, pleasure-loving . . . It began to ring a bell. Sixteen years back from 1942 brought us to 1926 . . . The bell clanged again. The husband's name was 'Amyas Crale' . . . The bell sounded a third time as I considered the initials A.C. – Archibald Christie. This third clang I judged to make the campanology more than coincidence.

I didn't mention my musings. It would have been more than anybody's life was worth to dwell on that disappearance. Even to light upon it for a moment with the glancing grace of a Camden Wonder.

STOP

Revelation Ahead

What did I think, Saunders wanted to know.

'There's one thing missing,' I said. 'A very important thing.' I didn't mean Christie, when you're as careful as I was being not to mention this and that, you end up suspecting your every remark as you make it.

'What?' he asked.

'The denouement,' I said. 'There's no denouement.'

'Yes there is,' he said – defensively, I thought.

'Ah, yes,' I said. 'But not what I mean, theatrically, as a denouement. There is no denouement *line*, no moment to make the audience gasp with sudden realisation. No "What did you do with the holster?" – no "*I'm* MacGregor!" In *Mousetrap* terms, no "I'm not a policeman . . . ".'

'What do we do?' asked Saunders.

'I'll tell you,' I answered. 'I don't know.' I thought I'd be honest. I went on: 'I'll have a go, you know me, I'll have a go. But I'm not at all sure it'll work.'

It half-did. I never cared for the trickery I resorted to, of having the accuser with his back to the killer and substituting a mere turn of the body (the accuser's) for the wanting slap-in-the-eye line of dialogue. But we were to take seven curtain-calls at the London opening night.

Revelation Ends

Go Back for Murder was a nightmare for the designer. And for the stage management. There were, nominally, six sets – five in the first act, one in the second. And six lots of furniture. The wee Duchess Theatre was surprised out of its scene dock. Let me explain – insofar as explanation is possible or even enlightening.

A girl, on her twenty-first birthday – in Canada again (a friend of old MacGregor's?) – opens a letter from her dead Mama. 'I didn't kill your father,' it reads. 'They all said I did and I did time for it but I'm innocent.' The girl comes to the Old Country to rake over that loose earth. (By this time a bit cakey.) Whence the five sets in Act One, she shops around among the people concerned. Each tells a different tale. In Act Two, we are in the Old House where everyone – and everything – is sixteen years younger. (An acid test for some of our Thespians.) The re-enactment will tell all.

Michael Weight who had designed the set for *The Unexpected Guest* designed the six for this one. Quite brilliantly, I thought. The first five were minimally sized, they had to be. It was a little like coming to the theatre to watch Television. We had more puzzles to offer than *What's My Line*, though.

I had a nice cast again. Led by Robert Urquhart. He played the solicitor who was engaged by the lass to walk her backwards through time. As written, the part was deadly dull. Robert and I were at pains to breathe life – even comedy – into him. The girl – a Canadian, remember – finds his office chilly. I wrote the following innocent exchange:

ROBERT: Do you find it cold in here?
GIRL: Your central heating is kind of low . . .
ROBERT: It's kind of non-existent, actually.

Not exactly S.J. Perelman. Nor did I mean it to be, I wanted a natural to-and-fro between a man who – in spite of himself – is fencing, even flirting . . . and a young girl from the other side of the world. Of the moon, as far as his Lincoln's Inn mentality might judge. Robert brought a lightness of touch and a charm to this legal sparrow that lifted him to heights I never thought the part could reach. It was such a long part, you see. It could have been lead. It was quicksilver. This meant, quite simply, the saving of the play on the first night in Edinburgh.

One of the easiest mistakes to make in assessing an actor's contribution is the confusion of part with performance. An indifferent actor will show up well in a good part. A good actor who pulls the author's chestnuts out of the fire to make a dull part shine bright, will often get little credit, even from a really discerning critic. Urquhart's contribution to our problem piece was never, I think, appreciated to the full by some.

The northern press were, in varying degrees, conscious of the difficulties I had done my best to surmount. In the *Daily Express*, under the headline 'ARTFUL AGATHA MAKES MURDER PAY – AGAIN' Robins Millar wrote:

> Agatha Christie missed her premiere of *Go Back for Murder* at the Kings Edinburgh staying far off in Karachi. Producer Peter Saunders could send her good news. This could be another profitable murder deal . . .

The writer adds, later: 'The play is one of the trickier Christies with a skill in hiding the thimble completely bewildering'.

The *Daily Mail* headline read: THERE'S JUST NO LOGIC, AGATHA. The notice ran:

> Agatha Christie fans will flock to see her latest, *Go Back for Murder* . . . It has the usual Christie ingredients and is well acted, well produced and thoroughly enjoyable. But for the first time I left a Christie play actually *annoyed* that I had not guessed whodunit.

> Normally one is perfectly happy to have theories and suspicions proved wrong by Miss Christie's logic. But I felt cheated by this one . . .

Another critic thumped the nail clean through the wall and out to the other side:

> Agatha Mary Clarissa Christie seems to have lost her corkscrew . . . the one she used with such effect to give those typical twist endings to her most successful mystery plays.
>
> This latest . . . is short of this one ingredient.
>
> Miss Christie has produced some 60 such crime pieces in book or play form varying on this basic formula. Here one wonders whether or not the variation imposes too much on director Hubert Gregg and his assistants.

The most unfortunate thing occurred just before the London opening. Not too unfortunate for Christie. It was announced in the press that she had sold the rights of all her works to MGM – except, of course, those in *The Mousetrap* – for the sum of one million pounds. Now people can take a certain amount of success in others . . . but there is a moment when quite another feeling than admiration creeps in. Not so much creeps as sweeps. It could be jealousy. The first night went very well indeed at the Duchess. The audience gave us prolonged applause at the final curtain. Peter Saunders who is never given to over-optimism – to expressing it, anyway – said as we made our way to the upstairs box for a glass of celebration: 'I think we'll get a year out of it.'

The critics were cooler than they had been in the north. Robert Muller came right out with what many people may have been thinking – surely irrelevantly: 'I don't care how rich Miss Christie is. This stinks'.

Next night I sat in a box at the back of the circle. The theatre was pretty full. But the most extraordinary sight met our inquiring gaze, Saunders' and mine . . . while they were waiting for the play to begin half the people in the circle held newspapers wide open, reading away at the notices. Or they may have been looking for a follow-up story on Agatha's million pounds.

I went backstage to have a word with my stalwarts. The piled up furniture in the wings looked as though an auction was about to take place. The thought passed through my mind that the whole would, in fact, be on sale before long. I thanked the cast. We had done our damnedest and come unstuck. Just why . . . who will ever know, who, in the theatre, ever does? I wish, though, MGM had paid Agatha the money quietly. In Karachi.

CHAPTER TWELVE
Rule of Three

I am invited to dine and break a garage door . . . For two gins I act every part in a play – one of three . . . Hanging and the whodunit . . . How to dress on a British beach and get an ovation for it . . . Agatha plays a part without an Equity card – and gets the sack anyway!

In the autumn of 1961 Peter Saunders asked me to dine with him at home. He had a house in the very exclusive Bishop's Avenue, Hampstead. (Not content with this ready-built house he began with, he later decided to have one built to his own specifications – and did do.)

He was always a perfect host. He gave parties every Christmas morning and I remember many a one of these. It irritated him that his guests were constantly mislaying their glasses (drinking) and having to be awarded clean ones. One Christmas I discovered, upon being given my first, that he had solved the problem. Those machines that print letters on coloured, sticky tape had just been invented. He had spent considerable time and energy playing with this new gadget, taping out the name of every guest. My wife, my brother Frank and I received our initial drinks in glasses prettily labelled 'Pat', 'Frank' and 'Hubert'.

As a matter of fact, Saunders always called me 'Humbert'. The reason for this went back to days when my name was quite often mis-spelt in newspapers – on occasions when it was included. There is a dictum among publicists that it doesn't matter what they say about you provided they spell your name right. In my case they hardly ever did. It went on for years. When young and ambitious I suffered being called most things, from 'Grieg' or 'Greig' to 'Gregory' or even 'Green'. 'Hubert' has come out as 'Herbert' (this was an obvious favourite), 'Hulbert' . . . even 'Hilbert'. And . . . 'Humbert'. I would telephone Peter in the early days of our acquaintance and announce myself as 'Humbert Greege'.

As *The Mousetrap* broke more and more records – or the main one by more and more performances – Saunders (wisely, I will always feel, I think in the same way) allowed himself pleasure after pleasure. He shared my liking for gadgetry. Once, when very young, I achieved a gramophone that changed its own records (not a new invention but mine was a Rolls Royce of a machine – it cost me £28 in 1938), a sunlamp, an electric razor (a very new invention) and a clock that woke me up in the morning by playing reveille. (Had I known that, within a couple of years, a bugle would be doing this I might have eschewed the clock.)

Peter acquired a pair of garage doors that opened when you operated a wireless what'sit inside the car. Today they are still a rarity in England. In America, they are as common as the push-button telephone. Everyone has them. And I've never known them to go wrong. In America.

My host drove me from the West End up to his house and prepared to show off the gadget. We sat in the car in his driveway . . . He pressed a button . . . and the garage doors opened like velvet curtains that revealed a Windmill nude. (It wouldn't have surprised me if he'd laid on something of that sort as a bonus. Gadget upon gadget.)

'That's marvellous,' I said. 'Now all you do is drive in . . . ?'

'All I do is drive in.'

'And they close behind you?'

'They close behind me.'

They did too. Velvet again. We continued to sit in the car. When a man is showing off a gadget you mustn't hurry him. You must be impressed and go on being impressed, it's expected. I had experienced all this Aladdin bit before, Saunders wasn't the only tycoon I knew. But I wasn't going to crack on. I can't bear spoiling anyone's fun, I hate it so if they spoil mine. I said:

'And when you want to drive out . . . ?'

'I do the same in reverse.'

'Do it,' I said. 'Let's drive out and in again.'

Saunders purred with satisfaction. He activated the mechanism, the doors silked open . . . He got into reverse and we moved back into the driveway.

Another activation . . . and the doors silked silently to a closure.

'It's that simple?'

'It's that simple,' he said. 'Better go in now, dinner won't be long . . . '

He activated again. There was a dreadful shuddering and the garage doors behaved as though they were in the hot seat in St Quentin – or wherever they keep it – and the electrician had slightly underdone the dose. They did everything but open. He tried again. Shudder, shudder . . . Was it that one of the earthquakes they're used to in Southern California had dared to pop up – or open – in Bishop's Avenue, NW? I'm not sure the skies didn't become overcast. After about the fifth go, we gave the doors best, got out of the car, left it in the driveway and high-tailed it into the house for a drink. We needed one.

Saunders got everything repaired the next day but I couldn't rid myself of the feeling that I had been to blame. Not for the first time, my kindness of heart, my – surely laudable? – desire to see everyone happy had brought disaster. I should have remembered. I should have warned Saunders that I tend to have a magically deleterious effect upon gadgets. Other people's gadgets – my own work a treat. (I had to sell those I mentioned to pay my war debts when I came out of the Army but they were all 'as new'.)

Once I went into a tobacconist's for cigarettes. (I've given them up, but not because of the following.) Gas lighters had come into vogue. I was still with petrol.

'That's one, is it?' I asked, innocently.

'Yes.'

The tobacconist picked it up to show me . . .

'Nice,' I said. 'Thank you' (pocketing my Players Mild and turning to go).

'Lights every time,' he said. 'Like this. Look . . . ' I did do and it did do. Fool, I rushed in . . .

'How do you fill it?' I asked. It wasn't this that did the damage; this was all right. He opened the thing, shoved a nozzle in it and squirted. Then I moved in for the kill.

'How do you change the flint?'

'Simple,' he said. He unscrewed something and a small but very strong spring shot up to the ceiling, hit it, came down again . . . and disappeared.

That's the end of the story.

The poor man got down on his hands and knees . . . the shop

began to fill with people . . . innocent people, all wanting their Players . . . and having to queue and wait. Because my built-in, natural gadget had had its usual effect of breaking up all before it.

It would have been fair to recall this for Saunders. I always forgot though. And gadgets everywhere fall to right and left of me as I walk through life, losing friends. Friends who like gadgets, that is.

I sat in Saunders' comfortable sofa (a far cry from the one I had lent him for *The Hollow*. There was no hole in the arm, for a start . . .) sipped my way into a huge gin and tonic and turned the pages of the script he had just given me.

It was a one-act play called *The Rats*. By Agatha Christie.

Rule of Three was the overall title. Three one-act plays. 'Will it work?' Saunders wanted to know.

I recalled the first play I had appeared in in London, at the Ambassadors' Theatre, it was. *Martine*. A beautiful poem of a drama by Jean-Jacques Bernard. Bernard's works are not well known in this country because of their length. Or shortness. They tend to play for about an hour and twenty minutes, we had to have a curtain-raiser before *Martine*. The play itself got the best press of any offering in years.

James Agate, noted as a strict critic, said: 'I do not always see eye to eye with Mr Carroll (Sydney Carroll, the presenter) in his productions. To this one I take off my best hat!

It didn't matter. We followed Agate's hat and came off after our one hundredth performance. The public didn't go for a split evening. At first we had a short – a very short – Bernard play as a curtain-raiser, then Mary Newcombe, the American actress, in the famous solo *La Voix Humaine*. Then . . . we came off. Noël Coward had made it with *Tonight at Eight-Thirty* . . . Or had he? Coward – for his own reasons – played a shorter run than *Martine*.

Would they take three from Christie? I said I thought it might depend on the three. *The Rats* I had read by now. It was a good enough melodrama. Acceptable. We tried it out then and there, I read the whole thing aloud, all four parts – Saunders cheered up visibly and we both had another gin. (I think dinner did come somewhere in the middle of all this. Whatever faults Saunders may have had, he was freer than Christie with the victuals. But I don't

ess shots of *The Unexpected*
uest. (The play Agatha
rely mentions in her
tobiography. We broke all
evious records at the
ıchess Theatre with a run
604 performances.)

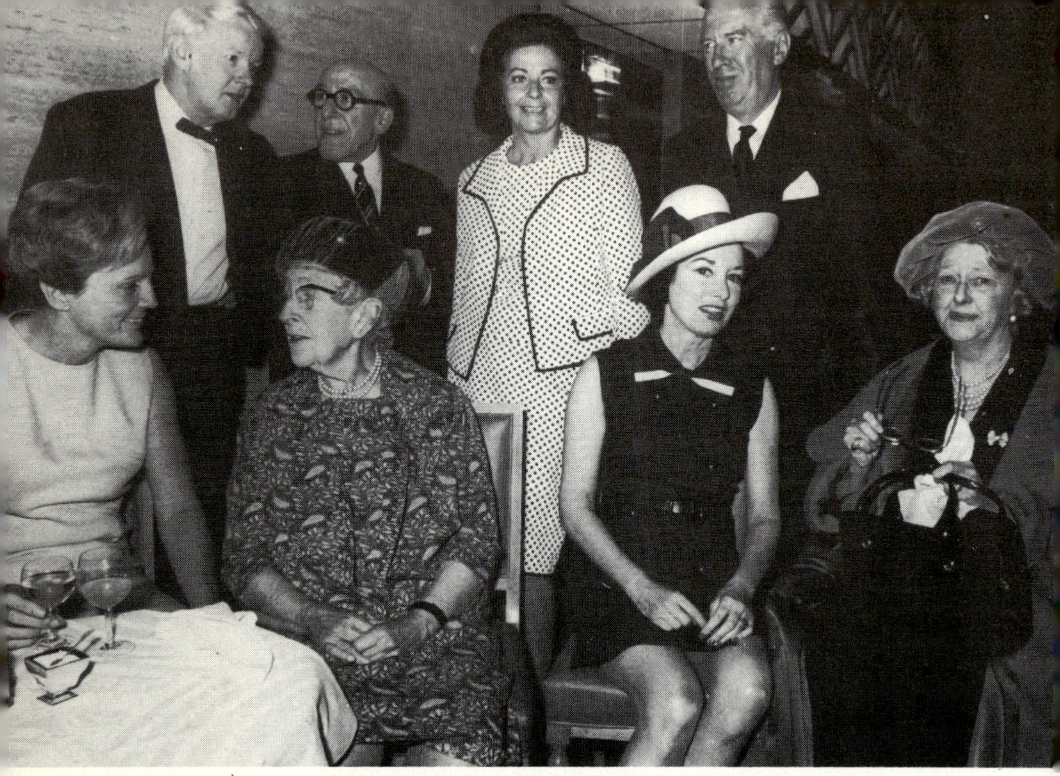

Saunders gave a luncheon at the Savoy for his General Manager, Verity Húdson. L to R, back row: the author, Robertson Hare, Margaret Lockwood, Peter Saunders. Front row: Miss Hudson, Agatha, Pat Kirkwood, Marie Löhr.

A press picture taken at the Dress Rehearsal of *Go Back For Murder* in Edinburgh. L to R, Nigel Green, Robert Urquhart, Lisa Daniely, the author, Ann Firbank.

recall eating. I just remember hamming away and having a melodramatic ball.

The Rats . . .

A couple of adulterers . . . one is an 'ess . . . are caught. Not in the act, but cornered. They can't get out of this one-room in a high-rise without doing a window leap. There's a body in a chest, too. It had tension, I'll say that for it.

Revelation Ahead

Of course, this is one of the Christie writings that, today, holds water like a colander. The squirming couple – the police are banging on the door and they'll be caught with the body – will be hanged. (Not with certainty because hanging was for the chosen few by then but the gallows did hover.) Today, they would get life – or less, ten years? Five with remission? Two if they're very bad and peers come to visit them and say, 'What a crying shame!' It may be all very nice for criminals, this encouragement we hand out to them at every do-good turn. But it plays hell with the whodunit. I mean, where do we go tomorrow? Who's going to gasp or even give a damn when Trotter in *The Mousetrap* is unmasked in the year 2000 if they know he's going to be let off with a caution?

Revelation Ends

Afternoon at the Seaside . . .

I had an affection for this little piece. It had the air of something got up by and for amateurs in the thirties – it could have won a prize at the Piddletrenthide Summer Festival. There were twelve characters, even I didn't essay this one solo, I read it at home.

Three bathing huts on a prom face us – one is even called 'Bide-a-Wee'. Below them, the beach. Full of the best of British on holiday. We, the audience, are the sea and I can only say that if this is the kind of view the Channel has been contemplating as it went in and out I can understand erosion.

But you couldn't go against the tide. As I saw it, there was only one way to direct this piece. Strictly for Piddletrenthide.

We have an expression in the theatre. 'In' or 'out'. 'In' means you leave it in the text or performance, 'out' means you cut it. I have a treasured memory of the auditions we held for *Rule of Three*. Honor

Blackman turned up. These were days when she had suffered under a film contract that wasted her considerable talents. And had not yet entered Bonding or Avenging. She marched on to the Ambassadors' Theatre stage with a script tucked under her arm. I greeted her at the orchestra rail. (I always make a point of doing this. Nothing, to my mind, is more lowering to the morale than to walk on to an empty stage in a near-empty theatre and address yourself to silent blackness. Any director who would put an actor to this torment – and humiliation – should be reduced to the ranks.)

'Good afternoon, Miss Blackman,' I said. (I adhere to politeness and respect, too, I'm old fashioned as hell.)

'Oh,' she said. 'Good afternoon.'

We knew that, having chosen actors with ability, we needed them to have versatility too. I decided to try Miss Blackman with a bit of the cockney lass on the beach.

'Would you mind,' I said, 'reading a bit from the second play?'

I got a puzzled look.

'*Afternoon at the Seaside*,' I said. 'It begins on page thirty-two.'

'My God!' said Miss Blackman. 'You don't mean to tell me that's still in!'

I don't know whether Christie heard. I can't think she didn't, she was sharp as a tack and she was sitting in the middle of the stalls. She didn't utter. Luckily I had my back to her. If I hadn't had she might have noticed two things. Firstly, that I had gone purple trying to choke down laughter. Secondly, that I had fallen in immediate love with Miss Blackman.

They are amiable people in this beach play. (There are no gallows hovering, by the way. Someone had done no more than pinch a necklace. Suspended sentence stuff.) They sunbathe, they bathe, they come out again . . . I would have loved to have Noreen (that was her name!) making her entrance, dripping, from the ocean-audience but we had to settle for her veering away as she approached the shore and arriving a hundred yards up the beach. Not the same. Noreen making a panting (and not dripping, we opened in Aberdeen in November and didn't want to lose her before London) entrance from Stage Right.

One critic saw exactly what I had been aiming at in directing the play.

His notice began:

> Well, well, Agatha, we never knew. All these years writing serious thrillers and then you come up with *Afternoon at the Seaside.* It is just as if you had sent us a naughty postcard from Brighton.
> *Afternoon* bears all the marks of that particular brand of rude, breezy humour and is, I think, the best part of *Rule of Three.*

I had indeed seen the play in the context of those postcards. I don't think Agatha had. She didn't complain at the result but she didn't thank me. I think she was even a little shocked at Noreen's undressing – and dressing – scene but she seemed to be happy enough at the laughter it evoked. And applause and even notices . . .

> Patricia Heneghan had the audience in fits as she changed from a swim suit to her frock.

> Patricia Heneghan got a round of applause all to herself for the manner in which she rid herself of her bathing costume and dressed herself with only a towel for a screen.

The above scene I decided to build up for just such a reception. There is nothing new about the crudity of undressing and dressing on a beach. Crudity made by prudery. The ungainly – and highly noticeable – contortions gone through by a person who is determined to be discreet. I proposed to present all this again. I felt it would fit this beach. It mightn't be as far as the Piddletrenthide Summer Festival was prepared to go but it would, I thought, be appreciable in London.

At the first excursion to the shops for wardrobe I found Saunders had budgeted for two bathing costumes for Noreen.

'We only need one,' I said.

He brightened. But said: 'What's she going to wear underneath when she takes it off, then?'

'Nothing,' I said.

Pat Heneghan, a super actress, both in comedy and out of it, contemplated the matter of being in a swim suit and out of it.

'Will it be all right?' she asked.

'It'll be great. Highly sexy, with absolutely nothing showing that shouldn't. And if you don't bring the house down I'll never speak to you again. I want you to get a bloody great round of applause for this piece of business or we'll both want to know the reason. It can't fail. Trust me.'

'Suppose I drop the towel?'

'Ah. There is that. Think of the publicity, though! Drop the towel . . . Now there's an idea . . . '

I wasn't serious. I knew exactly what I wanted to make of the scene. Sometimes it is possible in the theatre to create a five minute speciality. (The Americans call it a 'specialty', why bother with two more syllables? I have to admit that an exchange of dialogue such as that which occurs in the movie *Gold Diggers of 1933* wouldn't be happy carrying the extra syllabic weight. 'I want to do a specialty,' says Ginger Rogers. 'Sit down,' says Ned Sparks (whose looks always remind me, when I run the film in my wee cinema at home – it's the only recreation I have – of Peter Saunders), 'or you'll do a blackout.'

We rehearsed the scene in detail. 'I want nobody present,' I said, 'except the Stage Manager' (a chap) 'and the ASM' (a gal). Pat got into her swim suit, came on, and arranged her clothing in a heap at her feet. Noreen enlists the help of a bashful young man on the beach.

''Ere, 'old this,' she says (she's a cockney), giving him the towel and no chance to refuse. She has her back to us. While the boy is attempting to cover her she slips down her shoulder straps. Suddenly, she senses that the boy's holding the towel is going to be of no frontal help.

'Oh, give it to me!' she says and drapes it over her shoulders.

'Now what?' said Pat at rehearsal.

'Let me see . . . ' I said.

'What do you mean?' she said, leaning a little forward so that the towel would stay in place.

'I mean let me think.'

'All right but don't be long.'

I thought a lot, we both did. And we laughed a lot. The young ASM who was holding the script laughed too.

'I hope you're watching this closely,' I said to her.

'You're going to have to do it in a minute.'

'Me?'

'Yes, you. You're understudying Pat, aren't you?'

'Yes . . . '

'This kind of manoeuvre,' I said, 'has to be rehearsed within an inch of its life. One unsure move could mean disaster. Suppose Pat gets 'flu . . . '

'Thank you,' said Pat.

' . . . and you have to go on. Not enough to know your lines in this part. You have to know every move so that you could do it in the dark.'

'I'd rather do it in the dark,' she said.

'That's not what I mean. Now. Pat . . . '

'Yes?'

'Leaning slightly forward to keep the towel round your shoulders . . . '

'I'm doing that, yes?'

'Pull your bathing suit down to your waist . . . '

'Right.

And she did.

'I hope there won't be any stage hands upstage of me,' she murmured.

'There won't be. The Stage Director will see to that. Won't you?' I said to him.

'Of course.'

'In any case,' I said to Pat, 'you're leaning forward, the towel is covering you . . . Now . . . I want you to drop it.'

'What? Drop what?'

'The towel.'

'The towel? I shall be half naked!'

'Only at the front and you can cover yourself with your hands and arms. The back doesn't matter.'

'Right,' she said. 'Here goes.'

The towel fell. But the bathing suit wasn't low enough, it looked simply like a low back.

'That's no good,' I said. 'You look no ruder than you would in a frockless evening back.'

'Eh?'

'Sorry. Something I learned from the *Gay Cadets*. Before she could go into that, I went on:

'The bottom must be right down over the hips. So that the line is straight across – then we shall know you're rude in front.'

'I am rude in front,' she said.

'Maybe but you don't look it. Theatrically rude you're not.'

This – from the nakedry point of view – was as far as it was necessary to go. The rest was suggestion and the comedy ran fast. The boy puts the towel round her, then she asks for her bra. He picks it up off the beach and hands it to her. Leaning forward, towel draped over her shoulders, she gets into the bra . . .

'Wait a minute,' I said, 'what about the dialogue?'

We had ignored the script for some time. Dutifully, we checked. Nothing.

'Right,' I said. 'Your bra has been on the beach, it's sandy . . . '

'Christ,' said Pat.

'That's no good,' I said. I don't think she was suggesting it as a piece of dialogue, as a matter of fact. 'I've got it . . . "Blimey, it's full of sand!".'

'Is that my line?'

'It is now.'

'It is just as if you had sent us a naughty card from Brighton . . . ' the critic was to say, adding: ' . . . with Noreen Somers dressing on stage and all and saying in such a refeened voice as she straps on her brassiere "Oh, Blimey. It's full of sand".'

The next thing on is the dress over her head. Now we are down to the ridiculous wiggling and fumbling. 'Where's me drawers?' was another pearl of dialogue I added to the string. The drawers are small, mauve and transparent (but they go on under cover of the dress). Pat dealt superbly with moves and mutter. A final wriggle into this micro garment – Messrs Weiss of Shaftesbury Avenue got a round of applause at its very appearance, a sigh . . . and she turns, humming happily at the achievement. She deserved the ovation she got at every performance. Basic? Yes, but the play was basic. So was this particular facet of British beach life. To direct this piece along lines that excluded those – peculiarly British – post cards . . . would have been to run untrue to form.

I thought we might have a dog. One of the cast owned a poodle. Saunders paid it a few bob a week – or paid for its food or something, I don't remember. In return, this poodle was to be on call at every performance to walk from one side of the stage to the other. He managed without a pause.

One critic wrote: 'I liked . . . Hubert Gregg's direction, though I wish he would get rid of that silly poodle . . . '

Another wrote: 'There is also an engaging poodle; that alone seems to ensure a run of seven years.'

The third whodunit in the trilogy was called *The Patient.*

We have a paralysed wife in a did-she-fall-or-was-she-pushed conundrum. She has, the doctor announces, recovered a slight power of movement in the fingers and thumb of the right hand. She is able to compress a rubber bulb that activates a red light. One for yes, two for no. Was she pushed? – 'Yes' . . . Who pushed? . . . The doctor says he'll go through the alphabet. Luckily she stops him at 'B'. 'B' might be almost any of the suspects (Bryan, Brenda . . . Brother?)

Now the patient is left alone and the guilty 'B' will obviously have a go at finishing her off. In the dark. The Inspector and the doctor are waiting for this and on they come, putting up the lights. 'B' has already dodged behind a curtain.

The denouement – 'You can come out . . . ' (the Inspector adds the name) – wasn't bad. Not quite Edgar Wallace, though a touch in the tradition. Not exactly a bombshell to end the evening. A Roman candle. To end a sketch.

Agatha produced a staggering idea. One newspaper put it: 'Agatha Christie plays a trick on her audience – surely as novel a one as she has ever introduced . . . '

Another told more . . .

> Attempted murder. A whole group of suspects with perfect motives, a full quota of clues. But whodunit? That is what the recorded voice of thriller queen Agatha Christie asks at the end of the third playlet of her triple bill *Rule of Three* . . .

(We agreed to Agatha's making this record. She seemed convinced it would work and we wanted her to get it out of her system. On the first night, the voice – coming at the very moment of the denouement – caused a laugh, even a boo or two.)

> . . . And on the acuteness of Aberdeen audiences this week depends whether this problem ending remains as it is – or has to be changed to tell in so many words who did it.

'Who do *you* think is behind the curtain?' Saunders and I decided wouldn't do. It screamed, I thought, for the response, 'We've paid. *You* tell *us*!' The newspaper continued:

> A full report on how it was received will be sent to her this morning in Teheran where she is on holiday with her archaeologist husband by Peter Saunders who presents the show and Hubert Gregg who directs.

I don't think it was a full report but we said 'No'. In very little more than a word. I'm sure Saunders put it politely; he has beautiful manners. The first newspaper was disappointed:

> Alas, for my money they are going to change the ending for the rest of the week and reveal the culprit's identity!

The cast did well. Both casts, there was some re-shuffling before we reached London. All the actors had to play two or more parts. The difficulty of final choice lay in the acceptability of the doubling. A – who was jolly good as X and Y – made a less good job of Z. B was stronger as both Y and Z . . . Not so good when playing X, but wasn't X less important? Tricky decisions. Sad decisions. Trickier and sadder for me since I was also a fellow actor.

Rule of Three opened at the Duchess. As with *Go Back for Murder*, the sets filled the offstage area to the extent of forming an obstacle course for the players trying to make an entrance or an exit.

Betty MacDowell and David Langton (who would later make a TV name in *Upstairs, Downstairs*) were newcomers to the company and did more than well by Agatha. In all the plays by her that I directed I was struck by the extent to which the devices of 'up-casting' paid off. So many good actors were able to give the plays a quality that was not, I think, intrinsic.

The press views of *Rule of Three* differed widely. Firstly, a new and interesting viewpoint . . .

> The three one-act thrillers which constitute *Rule of Three* were written for the stage and not adapted from books.
>
> That makes them fresh thrillers for everyone . . .

(Not only 'fresh' thrillers for everyone but, for the director – I found, more dirigible.)

The plays were described by one critic as: ' . . . providing as rich and succulent a mixed grill as we've had in the theatre for a long, long time . . . '

The Scotsman, on the other hand, carried the headline: AGATHA CHRISTIE DISAPPOINTS – UNTHRILLING THRILLER'. (Did he leave after the first?) Following with:

> The offering consists of three one-act plays *with* [my italics] *no connecting link or theme to give the evening a sense of unity* and, as representations of Miss Christie's abilities, even her most ardent admirers must admit that they are sub-standard . . .

There followed something complimentary about me. Then the writer added:

> . . . but bricks cannot be made without straw and this commodity Miss Christie has surprisingly failed to provide.

CHAPTER THIRTEEN

Final Analysis

A lady loses her voice but keeps it quiet . . . Percy Marmont takes a party apart and Agatha rates a half-ton cake . . . A critic takes 'The Mousetrap' apart . . . An actress goes from Olivier to Christie and Hamlet is no longer playable . . . Agatha is honoured . . . and honoured.

Throughout rehearsals for *Rule of Three* I had stayed in London with my brother, Frank. He was, by day, a statistician for the Ministry of Energy – I think that's what it was, it used to be 'Power' but someone must have felt it wasn't a good name. (Has 'Energy' gone by the board now?) By night, he was a great theatregoer.

Pat was in Portugal supervising the building of the house I had designed. (I had never done anything of the kind before and made a bit of a balls of it. I thought yards were roughly the same as metres. Well, of course, they're not. When you get a room of ten metres it turns out to be not thirty feet but thirty feet, thirty inches. The house had six rooms and three bathrooms but looked like Citizen Kane's Xanadu. It cost like Xanadu by the time I had finished it.)

I wrote regularly and received regular replies in the form of progress reports. I telephoned too, but was put off this by letters which said: 'I have laryngitis, don't telephone, I can't speak to you . . .' 'Laryngitis getting better but slowly. Don't telephone . . . '

At last – the plays had just opened – she telephoned me. Her first remarks were as staggering as Christie's wheeze for not telling the audience what was going on. Pat hadn't told me, either.

'I'm only telephoning . . . ' she said in a barely audible voice, ' . . . because I'm all right . . . '

'What? All right, what do you mean "all right"?'

'There's nothing to worry about . . . I'm out of hospital . . . '

'Hospital?' I shouted. 'What hospital, what are you talking about?'

Slowly – and painfully – she told me the story. Some weeks earlier she had been involved – as a front-seat passenger – in a road accident. The car had been in collision with a lorry. She had been thrown forward and the lower part of her neck had hit the dashboard. The wound was within a millimetre or so – I didn't need to work that out – of her vocal chords. The specialist had told her she would probably never speak – certainly never sing – again. She had lain in bed in a nursing home in Faro, in pain, unable to eat, writing notes to communicate . . .

Had I known of course, I would have flown to her at once. Saunders, I'm quite sure, would have released me from the production. Pat, too, was sure of this and had accordingly sworn her friends to secrecy. After a few days – God knows how she managed it so soon but she did, to give me no inkling of trouble – she began again to write letters to me. They were full of cheerful, completely fictitious, accounts of how the building work was going, detailed descriptions. And requests to me not to telephone . . . I flew to Portugal the next day. I can't remember how much I told Peter, probably not the whole story. We didn't want to announce – even to friends – that Pat Kirkwood might never sing again.

It took a year or more. Gradually her speech returned. Then –one glorious morning . . . I was playing the piano in the upstairs drawing-room . . . downstairs I heard her begin to sing. Quietly at first but clear as a bell . . . The specialist, delighted with her determined progress had hinted that the singing voice might – in view of her willpower – one day come back. It wasn't to be forced. If she *wanted* to sing . . .

Today, she is singing better than before the accident. The voice has lost a couple of its highest notes but, in the lower register, has actually gained in strength.

By the time I was able to come back to London *Rule of Three* had ended its modest run. Agatha never wrote specifically for the stage again. Never again did I direct for her – nor for Saunders. I had withdrawn as director of *The Mousetrap* in, I think, 1960 . . . Somewhere around the time of *Go Back for Murder*. I had had seven years of it. I didn't want to go back there for any more murder. I didn't feel I could continue to bring anything new to it. It certainly wasn't bringing anything new to me.

On the seventh anniversary Peter Saunders threw a wing-ding at the Savoy. He invited a thousand or so guests – some eight or nine hundred of whom had never seen *The Mousetrap* and would have been inclined to look down their histrionic noses at it if they had. The idea seemed to be to bring the piece to more general notice and this end was achieved. The press, scorned and shunned by Agatha since December 1926, was being wooed by Peter Saunders on her behalf. And, of course, on his.

As you entered you were received by Saunders and Christie – neither of whom you could see because you were blinded by lighting. Your entrance was, it transpired, being recorded for newspaper, television and film – just in case you were important. If you weren't, there was always the long-odds chance that, dazzled, you'd fall flat on your invitation and make the front page that way.

I moved down into the body of the room and bumped into Percy Marmont among other chums. He expressed surprise at seeing me.

'Why?' I asked.

'I thought you'd be up there,' he said, pointing to the dais at the other end of the room. 'With the knobs.'

'I can't think of one reason why I should be,' I said. 'I'm not in *The Mousetrap*.'

'Sybil Thorndike is,' he said.

'In *The Mousetrap*?'

As a matter of fact, she'd have made not a bad 'Mrs Boyle'. A bit mannered but that could have been worked on.

'No, you fool. Up there. With the headmaster's lot.'

'Ah,' I said. I couldn't think of anything more. I had a glass of champers, then I said:

'As a matter of fact, who should be up there is Peter Cotes. He was the original director of *The Mousetrap* and I, for one, thought he did a bloody good job on it.'

'That's neither here nor there,' said Percy, letting himself go a bit. (And why not? My mother had cried her eyes out watching him in *If Winter Comes* at the Palace Theatre in the days when it was a bioscope. I think this kind of perenniality should carry privilege. I always thought old Percy should have got a CBE or the Freedom of the City or something for lifting Clara Bow out of that canoe . . .)

'Up on that dais . . . ' he perorated, 'are people who wouldn't touch the play with a barge pole, all lapping up the management's champagne . . . '

'Jolly good of him to provide it,' I said.

'Comes off tax,' said Percy.

'Don't we all?' I said. 'I bet the Maker shoves us all down as expenses.'

Agatha seemed to forget her legendary shyness of the press. At a peak moment she struck at a half-ton cake with a sword – Saunders guiding her hand, though I don't think she needed help – and smiled as though she thought she might get to eat it.

Like the disappearance, I don't suppose the mystery of the longevity of *The Mousetrap* will ever be solved. Eric Shorter, the distinguished critic, wrote after seeing the twenty-first anniversary performance:

> . . . Although Agatha Christie is not a name to be sneezed at, the play itself never struck its author . . . . . as having contained the seeds of immortality.
>
> Whether those seeds are to be found in the text or the performance, the theatre or its position, its management or its publicity, is a question which nobody can answer for sure. We know the manager is a keen and inventive publicist. Hence those huge cakes . . . [the more slicing she had to do, the more Agatha seemed to like it] club ties and other efforts to capitalise on the show's success. Mr Peter Saunders is the first to acknowledge that he has never missed a promoter's trick in keeping *The Mousetrap* baited.

Of the play and the performance of it, Shorter went on to say:

> The suspense, if not intense, is agreeable; and the plotting is unquestioningly neat.
>
> What is questionable is the quality of the acting which struck me as not rising to the proverbial level of rep. Most reps I know of could do better but of course they are not allowed to try – any more than a film can be made – until what Mrs Christie originally guessed might be 'quite a nice run' comes to an end. In our time? Our children's? Ever? Why in fact must the show go on? Only an Act of Parliament will ever stop it.

The quality of the acting may have deteriorated over the years. I can't believe a critic like Eric Shorter would have so spoken if it hadn't. I can only say that in my time I had some very talented boys and girls. Heather Stannard springs to mind. Olivier had chosen her for his production of *Venus Observed*. Out of the Christopher Frying pan into Christie, she may have felt was a strange move but she was a rattling good Molly. So was Mary Law. Pat Doonan, son of the unique Vaudevillian George Doonan, was one of the best Sergeant Trotters. Another Trotter was Ray Cooney who later bought the lease of the Ambassadors' Theatre. This led to the resetting of *The Mousetrap* next door at the St Martins'. A spoilt record. It is still an unbroken run but not at its original theatre. Ray can't be criticised. He went into management and that, in the theatre, means you're in wrestling where the holds aren't faked. When you cry out, it's for real.

Of all the critics, Eric Shorter saw *The Mousetrap* last . . . I put a further question or two and he was kind enough to answer:

Question: When did you last see *The Mousetrap*?

Answer: As it approached its twenty-fifth anniversary.

Question: Why do you think it has run so long?

Answer: Because it has run so long. It has a name for having run. It must have something to have run for so long. So one ought to see it – and, having seen it, one marvels that it should have run so long. A child can follow it. There is nothing thoughtful, serious, original or confusing – but it is also neat and complete and 'clean' for family viewing.

Question: Do you think it defensible that a play should should occupy a West End Theatre for so long?

Answer: Long runs are always artistically dreary but the shortage of small, attractive theatres in the West End (compared, for example, with Paris or New York) makes the occupation of, first, the Ambassadors' and, later, the St Martin's by an artistically uninteresting 'mystery' look exploitative. Would it have run at one of the bigger theatres?

The anomaly continues to be. At the moment of writing no 'Act of Parliament' has been passed. It isn't even on the Statute Book.

Shakespeare – per me (and Anthony Hicks?) – gave it a name. Christie's gain has been, considerably, Shakespeare's loss, I'd say. I'm glad that it was in the year 1950 – or 2BM (Before *Mousetrap*) –

that I played Hamlet. I'd hate to play him today. I mean, you can't leave out the line, that would be the ultimate in humiliation for the poor old Bard. But how would you get past:

> King: What do you call the play?
> Hamlet: The Mousetrap . . .

I defy the Dane not to get a laugh. Tremendous advertisement, of course. Not in the classic tradition. But then . . . no more is *The Mousetrap*.

Questions remain. Questions will always remain. Without the disappearance would the Agatha Christie name have acquired the devastating box office magnetry that overrides the need for actors of note, even for actors? What had she – as a writer on the page – that put her above . . . Margery Allingham? Dorothy L. Sayers? These, in their field, have been called writers of quality. If the word has been used in connection with Agatha Christie I have missed reading the criticism. She held a Doctorate of Letters (Honorary) and a Fellowship of the Royal Society of Literature. After four stage triumphs, in the New Year's Honours of 1956, she was made a Commander of the British Empire.

Agatha Christie is, we know, tremendously readable. Are others less readable because they bear other names? With fewer letters after them? It has been explained that she had 'the common touch' without which you may never go great guns at the box office. Was the 'embroidery' of which Simenon spoke so scathingly just the job for those who led unembroidered lives?

There is no question whatever, in my mind, that the Christie disappearance was unintended as a catcher of publicity for her books. To give publicity to Archie, to make his life a misery, yes. But Agatha had no thought that she should gain. Or suffer. In purely financial terms 'suffer' is, of course, not the word at all. Her fortune – carefully distributed so that it would attract minimal posthumous tax – was estimated finally at somewhere (does it matter just where?) between fourteen and twenty million pounds. It was said that she made more out of poison than Lucrezia Borgia.

In common with other multi-millionaires Agatha showed herself to be thrifty to the point of parsimony. She may well have given much to charity without letting the fact be known – following one of the best but least attractive poetic guidelines ('Do good by stealth and blush to find it fame'). If so she had quite a bit left over.

Postamble

It was a fascinating experience to meet and know Agatha Christie. A legendary lady. It is given to few to delight the world and we honour her for this.

In my professional dealings with her – and there were not that many others – I found her to be shrewd and a trifle ruthless. Insensible, a touch vain – and contained. She was very contained.

All the above are professional pluses. Success to the extent that she achieved it is not a thing of softness and amiablity.

She was – and this too comes into the 'professional' category – short on appreciation. She owed an enormous debt to Peter Saunders yet in her autobiography she gives him scant mention. Speaking of *The Hollow*, she says merely that it was a success. (If it hadn't been it is doubtful whether *The Mousetrap* would ever have been set. And the way paved for later success and advancement.) Speaking of *The Unexpected Guest* she says quite simply that she wrote it. I think perhaps she didn't like to confess – to herself, even – that her theatrical accomplishments could not be achieved without help.

She never expressed thanks to the press for the help she gained from them. Some of their attention may have been unwanted but the help came flooding. They had bulleted not only her name but the very word 'mystery' to the forefront of common notice. Such was the force of the discharge and so ready the supply of ammunition for shot after follow-up shot that she has remained in the forefront. She has defied changes of taste, sharpenings of critical view, the breaking of New Waves. She is a mighty anomaly. A square peg in a round world.

Long may she continue to baffle the reader. Even the theatregoer, though there the squareness of the peg may, today, be found to let in the draught.

(Not in the case of *The Mousetrap*. That goes on, at the time of writing, though the wind may whistle and some voices howl.)

In 1968, Max was knighted and Agatha became Lady Mallowan. Three years later she became Dame Agatha in her own right. She died on January 12th in 1976.

In response to my letter of condolence I received a request for a contribution to an Agatha Christie Memorial. I had, I thought, made one. In any case, what more fitting memorial than *The Mousetrap*? May it outlast the memory of the disappearance. And close with honour.

A final thought. The rest of that quotation from *Hamlet* . . . After:

> KING: What do you call the play?
> HAMLET: The Mousetrap . . .

the Prince goes on a bit about the plot, then he says: 'Tis a knavish piece of work. But what o' that . . . ?'

We are reminded, comfortingly, that Hamlet, theatre-lover though he may be, sees no objection to a play serving a purpose.

INDEX

Index